# STATUS AND POWER IN VERBAL INTERACTION

# Pragmatics & Beyond
# New Series

40

Julie Diamond

*Status and Power in Verbal Interaction*

# STATUS AND POWER
# IN VERBAL INTERACTION

## A STUDY OF DISCOURSE
## IN A CLOSE-KNIT SOCIAL NETWORK

JULIE DIAMOND

JOHN BENJAMINS PUBLISHING COMPANY
AMSTERDAM/PHILADELPHIA

TM The paper used in this publication meets the minimum requirements of American National Standard for Information Sciences — Permanence of Paper for Printed Library Materials, ANSI Z39.48-1984.

**Library of Congress Cataloging-in-Publication Data**

Diamond, Julie.
    Status and power in verbal interaction : study of discourse in a close-knit social network / Julie Diamond.
        p.      cm. -- (Pragmatics & beyond, ISSN 0922-842X ; new ser. 40)
    Includes bibliographical references and indexes.
    1. Discourse analysis--Social aspects. 2. Sociolinguistics. 3. Power (Social sciences) I. Title. II. Series.
P302.84.D5      1996
306.4'4--dc20                                                                                              96-4154
ISBN 90 272 5052 9 (Eur.) / 1-55619-801-9 (US) (alk. paper)                          CIP

John Benjamins Publishing Co. • P.O.Box 75577 • 1070 AN Amsterdam • The Netherlands
John Benjamins North America • P.O.Box 27519 • Philadelphia PA 19118-0519 • USA

# Table of Contents

# Acknowledgments

First and foremost, I would like to thank Professor Richard Watts at the University of Berne for his careful supervision, useful criticisms and much needed advice during all phases of this work, from inception to completion.

I am extremely grateful to Dr. Arnold Mindell, whose own research serves as a valuable inspiration, and who has given so freely of his support and friendship. I owe an enormous thanks to Dr. Joseph Goodbread for many stimulating and provoking discussions which have contributed to this work.

The original manuscript was helped along by Leslie Heizer's editing skills, and the technical support of Kate Jobe and Peter Jakob. Thanks go to Stan Tomandl, Robbie Miller and Lee Jones for their help with the final manuscript. I am most grateful to Tim Anderson for his generous help in preparing the manuscript for publication.

My deepest thanks go to the members of the community whose conversations, meetings and parties I taped for two years, and who allowed me to pry into their activities, judgments and perceptions. Finally, I thank Richard and Nancy Diamond, whose love and support have enabled me to pursue my interests, and to whom I dedicate this work.

# Chapter One: Introduction

## 1. Goals and overview

Casual conversation, the stuff of everyday social life, appears effortless, informal and at times superficial. Yet many of our social interactions are enacted through conversation. An awkward encounter, a disagreement between conversational partners, and we feel as if a whole system has gone awry. People's behavior in ordinary conversation is not as random as it sometimes appears, but reflects the social structures in which the momentary conversation takes place, as well as the nature of the participants' relationships to each other. Behavior not only constitutes but perpetuates the larger social structure. Each interaction adds another strand to the web of social structure, holding in place the individual's role, the statuses of the participants and the relationships between them.

Without much effort we can see that everyday talk is orderly: people talk more or less one at a time, things get said and then done, themes follow each other with greater or lesser degrees of coherency, etc. This orderliness of conversation must result from implicit or unconscious rules of organization, which we shall call constraints. There have been many attempts to postulate what these constraints must be, attempts to find the rules behind the surface regularities and order. Some attempts focus on the organization of talk, others on the social variables concerning the interactants, the settings, and the goal of the talk. Some of the constraints we will focus on in this study are the constraints of social relations, power, status and the demands of maintaining on-going relationships, demands which we will devote more time to in coming chapters, but which may be summarized here as the need to balance self-presentation with group-membership.

One main premise here is that people maintain their social structures through talk; the rules governing talk are rules governing the relationships between people. Thus, the constraints on talk are the constraints on social relationships. What are the constraints on social relationships? They are the constraints of power, status and intimacy. People are constrained in their talk by the kinds of relationships they have to their conversational partners, i.e., whether they are friends and acquaintances, status equals, inferiors or superiors. Relationships are also constrained by the type of situations the participants are engaged in, whether they are at a party, a meeting, in school or at work.

Using an ethnographic analysis of the dynamics of social interaction, we will study the ways in which social relationships are established and maintained through discourse. The social structure of one particular social organization, a training institute for psychotherapy, will be analyzed through the verbal interactions of the members. The specific group under observation consists of practitioners and students of psychotherapy. The conversations which were recorded are not, however, therapeutic conversations, but activity-centered conversations of meetings and discussions, and everyday chats and conversations between participants. This work is not an attempt to uncover the regularities and principles of therapeutic discourse; that has been dealt with elsewhere and would constitute another study (cf. Labov and Fanshel, 1977; Lakoff, 1989). Instead, I am using this group to see how people use conversational strategies, linguistic devices to mark out social and interpersonal meanings and relationships.

The therapists and students are members of a training institute, a community that Gumperz (1989) would call a "community of the mind," as opposed to a "community on the ground." It is a group of people held together by common interests, ideas, goals and tasks, rather than by a physical locality such as a neighborhood, village or region. This particular community is representative of a type of political, social or educational group consisting of people who are linked together by their identification with a set of ideals. While sociolinguists in the earlier part of the century conducted research on groups bound by regional and historical bonds, a growing phenomenon in the latter part of this century is the study of groups of people held together by ideas, common interests, tasks and beliefs.[1] Due to the rise of telecommunications technology, we are ever more influenced by non-local groups: religious groups, ethnic groups, and political organizations such as the environmental, ethnic, antiwar and antinuclear movements in Europe and America. Even many ethnic groups, who, due to political and economic upheavals, can no longer be identified with a physical locality are becoming progressively

---

[1]    cf. Harman (1988).

more linked to each other through a shared set of ideologies, ideas, beliefs and practices.

The borders between communities on the ground and communities in the mind are fuzzy; ethnic groups, for example, which have typically been studied as communities with physical localities, such as African-Americans, also share properties with communities of the mind. African-Americans are linked first and foremost through a shared identity rather than through a shared locality. Though locality plays a part in studying local networks of African-Americans, we can witness similar linguistic forms of the Black English Vernacular (BEV) whether in Chicago, New York, Houston or Los Angeles. Another example of a community of the mind are women, who have been the target of numerous studies on language use and conversational style. These communities of the mind have specific problems and issues that have impact in the fields of sociology, psychology and linguistics.

## 1.1. The analysis and interpretation of culture

Interpreting the activities of a socio-cultural group and unraveling its social structure touches upon sociology and ethnology as well as linguistics. In fact, this is an ethnographic work in the sense that we are "construing social expressions on their surface enigmatical" (Geertz, 1973). The analysis of culture is an interpretive task, for what appears on the surface of a given culture are enigmatic, ritualized and meaning-laden behaviors that we must interpret in order to understand the culture and the matrix of meanings between speakers. Geertz says that the ethnographer

> is faced with...a multiplicity of complex conceptual structures...which are at once strange, irregular, and inexplicit ... Doing ethnography is like trying to read (in the sense of "construct a reading of") a manuscript-- foreign, faded, full of ellipses, incoherences, suspicious emendations, and tendentious commentaries, but written not in conventionalized graphs of sound but in transient examples of shaped behavior (1973:10).

The "transient examples of shaped behavior" of this group are talk. It is the way individuals talk, how they manage conflicts, come to resolutions, interrupt each other, get the floor, raise topics and tell stories. This verbal behavior is enigmatic in that it is full of ellipses, gaps and

holes. Meanings which are implicit to the group members are often
abbreviated and thus indecipherable for the observer. Meetings are
adjourned, decisions made and projects undertaken without any explicitly
assigned leader or facilitator.

Finally, this work employs the ethnographic method of participant
observation. The investigator is a part of the group under observation, is
on the scene as a participant and as an observer. As Kochman states,

> [t]his is premised on the well-founded view among linguists and anthropologists
> that the patterns of language and culture are best seen and understood within the
> context in which they originate and develop or are in regular use (1981:3).

The type of research in which the observer is simultaneously a
participant, or at least accepted by the speakers, has been a growing trend
in sociological and anthropological research at least since the 1930s,[2] but
has only come to prominence in sociolinguistic research with Gumperz
and Hymes' (1964, 1972) ethnography of communication and Labov's
(1972a) study of BEV in New York City. Realizing that access to the
vernacular would be difficult if not impossible were he merely to
interview speakers, Labov chose to spend some months, together with
two other black fieldworkers, "hanging out" with gang members. Labov
rarely interviewed the speakers alone, but would, for example, interview
two boys at a time, so that he was "outnumbered" and not dominating the
interview situation. Furthermore, he would ask questions that elicited
stories, not just single-word answers, and the boys frequently forgot
about Labov and ended up talking to each other. Where other linguists
and educators had failed (cf. Bereiter, Engelman, et al. 1966), Labov,
using these and other techniques, was able to gain access to the Black
English Vernacular. The traditional interview situation, in which
generally a white adult male interviews a young black child in a location
outside of the boy's or girl's own neighborhood is such an inherently
unnatural situation for the child that a rich corpus of verbal data could
never be obtained under such circumstances. Labov points to this as the
reason why (generally white) educators have concluded that black
children are verbally deficient.

Cheshire (1982), Milroy J. (1981) and Milroy and Milroy (1978) all
found that access to the vernacular was only possible through access to
the network. In this study, the speakers were only minimally aware that

---

[2]   cf. William F. Whyte's (1943) classic study of street corner society.

they were being recorded. As Milroy L. (1987) points out, it is difficult for speakers to keep in mind the fact that they are being recorded. Another major factor here is that a group, not an individual, was being recorded. Thus, the strength of the group dynamics overrode the individual participant's awareness of the recorder. As L. Milroy states:

> [T]he tendency of outside observation to encourage careful, standardized styles and inhibit the emergence of vernacular structures is to a considerable extent counteracted by the operation of the group dynamics (1987:63).

That the researcher is a participant in the group and was present at many of the meetings and discussions is a factor which does have an influence on the interpretation of the data. In fact, it is a benefit, for she has insight into the group members, can discuss the extralinguistic social features of the members, and can use her ability to recall the group dynamics, atmosphere and overall situation of the recorded speech event.

## 1.2. Discourse structure and strategies

As a study of social interaction through language, this work will use the tools of discourse analysis. Discourse analysis is an area of linguistics which, like pragmatics and sociolinguistics, is concerned with language in use. Attempts to define or delineate this large, somewhat new and interdisciplinary field are numerous and invariably betray the researcher's own difficulty in navigating the theoretical morass. Consider for example Schiffrin's (1987) opening sentence on discourse analysis: "Discourse analysis is a vast and ambiguous field." Brown and Yule (1983) have a similar difficulty in the opening of their book on discourse analysis: "The term 'discourse analysis' has come to be used with a wide range of meanings which cover a wide range of activities." Stubbs (1983) is a little more to the point in his attempt to define the field: "The term discourse analysis is very ambiguous." One reason for the difficulty in defining discourse analysis is its interdisciplinary nature. It is only partially a linguistic discipline, but touches upon sociology, anthropology, semiotics, ethnography, psychology and philosophy. The different dimensions of discourse analysis can be seen as different foci on the same entity. Like the proverbial five blind men touching the different parts of the elephant, each believing that he indeed possesses the true nature of the elephant, so too discourse analysts differ as to what they believe discourse analysis is.

For our purposes, we can best define discourse analysis by its scope: studies of discourse have in common their interest in either 1) language in use, including its functions, the speakers, diversity of speech, ethnography of speaking, and social factors correlating with speech; and/or 2) language above the sentence level, including cohesion in text and discourse, interaction, the structure of verbal exchange, text production and comprehension. Thus, the different approaches to discourse which abound today result from the different foci; one can focus on the text itself, on the speaker interaction, the structure of talk, the function of the utterance, or the relationship of the speaker's social features to the text, to name just a few possibilities.

Discourse analysis is a branch of pragmatics, the study of meaning situated in context. Pragmatics, or the philosophical study of language function or language as action, was brought into modern linguistics by the works of Austin (1962), Grice (1975) and Searle (1969, 1975). The meaning of an utterance is its function, how it is used in a particular context. Austin saw utterances as actions and defined a set of speech acts which people use to perform actions. For example, requests, commands, promises, threats or apologies are all speech acts. Any given utterance can be not just one but a combination of several speech acts. Pragmatics is chiefly concerned with the relationship of the speaker to the utterance. Discourse can be seen as a multileveled matrix of meanings in which speakers are not merely conveying information, but are performing actions which constitute social life.

Other traditions of discourse analysis focus on the discourse as a text, either written or oral. Textlinguistics, stemming from the European discipline of "Textwissenschaft," is an area of discourse analysis concerned with the text as the object of study, the relationships within the text, and the relationship of the speakers to the text. Interest here is in text production and comprehension, and the cohesion and understanding of text. Other foci of discourse analysis are on the speakers and the interaction between them. There are those who study the structure of the conversation, attempting to understand the rules and regularities which guide participants in their verbal exchanges. Others focus on the relationship between the participants and the social context in which the interaction is embedded. There are those who study how speakers use language diversity and the many possible speech varieties that exist to convey social meanings.

For the study undertaken here, we are mainly concerned with the areas of discourse analysis which study the structure of spoken discourse and speakers' interactions. More on discourse analysis, its history, development and role within linguistics will be presented in Chapter 2, "Language in Context," and the specific discourse structures and strategies that will enable us to analyze and interpret spoken interaction will be shown, together with the data, in Chapters 3, 4 and 5. For now, it is important to introduce briefly two concepts of discourse analysis that will elucidate the central thesis of the work.[3]

The ethnographic paradigm of Goffman (1959, 1967), Hymes (1962) and others, concerned with the interpretation and analysis of everyday social events, led to the study and formulation of rules that govern linguistic behaviors such as taking turns in conversation (Sacks, Schegloff and Jefferson, 1974), interruptions, code switching (Gumperz, 1972, 1982), and indirect and polite speech forms (Lakoff, 1973, 1975; Leech, 1983; Brown and Levinson, 1978, 1987). These studies of the structure of social interaction reveal information about the social relationships of the speakers, as well as the situation in which the interaction takes place.

Goffman (1981) and Hymes (1962) suggest a metacommunicative component to language; utterances contain frames. Every message is sent along with a set of "instructions for use." The metacommunicative part of the message signals options for interpretation, and is usually, but not exclusively, transmitted through prosodic and nonverbal cues which Gumperz (1982) has referred to as contextualization cues. These frames or metacommunications are as necessary for understanding the message as is the semantic content, for they tell the communicative partner how to interpret the message. Frames can refute or contradict the message part, and often signal non-linguistic information, generally of a social or psychological nature, for example, social features such as class, status,

---

[3] For more detailed reviews of discourse analysis see Teun van Dijk, 1985; Schiffrin, 1987; Brown and Yule, 1983; Stubbs, 1983; and for an historical overview see Gumperz and Hymes, 1972.

relationship to the listener, etc., or psychological features such as emotional state, affect, etc.

Sometimes these frames, or metacommunications, can be communicated through the actual structure of the discourse, specifically in the ways speakers negotiate the interaction, creating strategies out of the structure. The nature of verbal interaction has been perhaps most clearly set forth in the seminal work of Sacks, Schegloff, and Jefferson (1974), where they posit a system that could "generate" well-formed conversations, based on the dynamics of turn-taking. According to Sacks et al. interactants in a verbal exchange are constrained by the rule of one speaker at a time.[4] This constraint has the effect that turns in conversation proceed more or less smoothly, and that there is a minimum of simultaneous speech. Participants take turns speaking and thus negotiate the floor through the principle of "current speaker selects," that is, the current speaker either self selects, selects the next speaker or fails to select, in which case the floor is open to any bidder. Their system accounts for how speakers manage potentially difficult conversational areas such as interruption, overlapping and simultaneous speech, silence and speaker selection.

The analysis of the verbal interaction in Chapters 3, 4 and 5 will show the dynamics involved in managing personal relationships and what it entails for individuals and groups. By extracting these dynamics we will be able to see the larger social structure of the institute, the verbal strategies its members use, and the ways in which members achieve political effectiveness. It is not a quantitative study that is being attempted here, nor is it a study where the findings can be extracted and applied to other groups. Rather, the type and object of inquiry - the management and negotiation of interpersonal relationships within a cultural context and how relationships define and illuminate the larger social structure in which the relationships take place - can be carried out in other cultures to discover more about the nature of relationships and interaction.

---

[4]    This observation needs to be tested cross-culturally. White, European-American conversational style can be said to proceed according to the rule of "one speaker at a time;" however, simultaneous, overlapping speech is characteristic of other cultural styles.

## 1.3. Power and status

Within any community, whether a community of the mind or a community on the ground, members are segregated according to certain factors. There are specific factors of every institution, such as experience, seniority, rank in the organization, and external social factors such as sex, social class and race. There are also factors internal to the organization that are not immediately available to the observer which contribute to the hierarchy of a community. As we shall see in this study, institutionalized status alone does not account for the relative power and political effectiveness of the members.

### 1.3.1. Status and Rank

For the purposes of the study, we shall define status as rank ascribed to individuals either on the basis of birth (such as sex, age, nationality, race) i.e. without reference to abilities, or achieved through individual effort. I shall use the term *rank* instead of *status* for the following reasons. Status implies social stratification on a vertical scale. An individual's status, his or her place in the social order, based on sex, age, family relationships, occupation, economics, marital status, education and other factors is more or less fixed; one's status as a woman, man, black, white, poor or rich, etc. changes only as the culture changes. There is not much an individual can do to contest the status given to these fixed, external variables. In some cultures, individuals can change status through effort and competition, but the meaning given to each particular social stratum is fixed by the cultural consensus and views.

Because status implies a fixed, external social variable, the concept does not take into consideration contextual dependency. For instance, what is accorded high status in one culture may not be accorded the same status in another. Cooks may be accorded high status in one culture and lower status in another culture. Worldwide, men are given higher status than women, but there are certain societies and sub-cultures where woman enjoy higher status than men. Yet these societies or sub-groups still take place in the larger world where woman have lower status. Thus, sometimes status within a given context overlaps or even contradicts fixed, external status. In a university setting, for example, an African American female professor supervises a white, male graduate student.

They are close in age. Within the university setting, the professor has institutional rank over the student. But in the world at large, a white male has much greater status than an African American female. How do these two facts intermingle? What type of interaction arises from this overlap of status? Does one take precedence over the other?

If we examine this phenomenon more closely, we see that the contextually dependent status and the fixed, external status are qualitatively different. The fixed, external variable is less likely to change. The only change that can occur to lessen the social difference between these two is not up to the individuals alone, but rather up to the culture. Age, race, sex, nationality cannot be altered; only the stigma or privilege associated with these variables, and upon which the stratification is based, can change. The variables won't change, but the cultural meaning ascribed to them changes as the culture changes. On the other hand, certain contextually dependent variables can be changed through individual efforts. The male graduate student can, theoretically at least, with effort, become a professor some day. In a business, a salesman can, through hard work, some day become vice-president in charge of sales. In a street gang, a younger member can one day become a leader by impressing others with fighting skills. This is very different from race, nationality, religion, sex, i.e. those variables that cannot be contested; only the meaning associated to them can be contested, as through social action.

Thus, I propose that we use a different term that will highlight these important differences. Let us call status, then, *rank* and differentiate *institutional rank* (or universal rank) from *local rank*. Institutional rank consists of those external, more or less universal, fixed social variables, some of which are acquired at birth, such as sex, nationality, race, and some of which are acquired through effort, such as education and occupation. Local rank consists of those social variables whose meanings are internal to a particular community. A good example of local rank is found in Labov's (1972) description of gang members' rank in terms of their participation in certain activities which are accorded high status in that group, for instance, raising pigeons and fighting. Local rank includes the degree of belonging to a particular group, and integration into that group, or what is commonly referred to as popularity. Popularity is meeting the social requirements of a particular group, resulting in a high degree of integration into the group. Institutional rank is macrolevel rank, much of which is universally agreed upon. Local rank is the subjective assignment of value based on the local community's ethos.

As we shall see in this study, breaking down these two aspects of status into institutional and local rank has implications for power in discourse. In the data, we see that local rank is contested and vied for in conversation; it is this level of rank which is most "up for grabs." In discourse, when people bid for the floor, compete, negotiate roles in conversation, interrupt each other, etc., they are vying for local rank. While institutional rank permeates and affects roles in discourse, the actual institutional rank of each member cannot be contested through discourse. No amount of taking the floor, interrupting, raising topics, etc. will ever equalize the inequality between black and white, men and women, in the culture at large. But in the local community, the battle for equality and for power is waged at the level of local rank.

### 1.3.2. Power and Rank

What, then, is the role of power in relation to rank? Most studies approach power and status from a macrolevel analysis, and see power as an attribute associated with institutional rank. This study shows, however, that power is not determined by institutional rank or external variables alone. Although hierarchies are created and enforced by social norms and institutional status, the data show that individuals can and do contest power and compete for leadership roles in every verbal interaction. That participants argue, disagree and compete for the role of speaker points to the fact that power is more than a property invested in individuals by society or by an institution.

This study is a microlevel analysis of power and rank: the way power and rank between interactants is negotiated through conversation. Such an analysis, is, I believe, an important auxiliary to existing macrolevel studies of power. There is often a perceived antagonism between microlevel and macrolevel studies of power; it is beyond the scope of this work to reconcile these two approaches here. Perhaps it is even naive to assume that these two views can ever be reconciled once and for all. It may well be that both approaches to power need to exist side by side, augmenting and reflecting each other. In situations where institutionalized rank is assigned to a group on the basis of race, nationality, sex, religion or other social variables, it is essential to include the macrolevel aspects of power in the analysis. A microlevel analysis is useful in its ability to find how interactants negotiate roles and exert influence in situations where they are in the typically "weaker" role. As we shall see, interactants, regardless of institutional rank, use strategies to contest, dispute and resist the roles assigned to them. The microlevel analysis shows power as an ability accessible to all interactants. The microlevel approach has important social and ethical uses, for it shows how interactants use communicative competence and creativity regardless of their assigned social or institutional roles. In much the same way that Labov (1972) helped to show the richness and creativity of Black English, disproving the claim that it was merely a random collection of features deviating from standard English, a microlevel analysis of power can help discard the cultural bias against those in lower social positions by showing that, though they may be politically and socially disempowered, they still have options and abilities to assert their position, to reject the roles assigned to them, and to exercise political effectiveness in interaction.

I use the terms *political effectiveness* and *power*[5] interchangeably for the following reasons. Power is political and rhetorical; we witness an individual's power, for instance, in his or her ability to win an argument, to introduce a new topic, to bring across a reform, to change existing structures, to lead a discussion, to hold sway over others, to become elected or nominated for a position, etc. By defining power as political effectiveness we are stressing the fact the power is not merely a quality which is assigned or earned; it is also an interactional *skill* and *process*. Power is the skill that all members have to contest roles, dispute, and disagree on the interpretation of events. Power is a process insofar as the participant in an interaction who attempts to exercise power needs to be ratified and accepted by the other interactants. Though people will follow or agree on the surface with what a leader says, disobedience, defiance and even hostility can be conveyed through a number of covert means. For those who have taught or have been in a position of authority, nothing is more aggravating than the allusion of compliance and a

---

[5]   For an excellent and concise review of the various approaches to power in sociology, see Lukes (1974).

background of negativity. Nothing deflates a leader more than being followed reluctantly.

In what Dahl (1957) calls the "intuitive idea of power," power is the ability of person A to get person B to do something against person B's will. However, this definition is unsatisfactory on two accounts. First, it is a view of power that explains coercion and violence rather than the very subtle exercise of power that one witnesses, for example, in getting someone to accept one's view, to take one's belief as one's own, or to agree with a given interpretation of reality. Coercion cannot change minds. I am interested in what changes minds, and what changes group minds, as well. Along these lines, then, our definition of power is more akin to that of Bachrach and Baratz who state that not only is power the ability of Person A to get Person B to do something against Person B's will, but

> [p]ower is also exercised when A devotes his energies to creating or reinforcing social and political values and institutional practices that limit the scope of the political process to public consideration of only those issues which are comparatively innocuous to A (1970:7).

In other words, power is not just the ability to coerce someone or to get them to do something against their will, but rather, it is the ability to interpret events and reality, and have this interpretation accepted by others. Power is therefore, in the words of Schattschneider (1960), "the mobilisation of bias. Some issues are organised into politics while others are organized out." The powerful member of a community is not the one who "plays the game and wins," but the one who makes up the game's rules. This is thus political effectiveness, as seen in effective rhetoric and politic behavior.

An additional reason institutional rank is insufficient as a sole determinant of power is that it does not take into account the dynamic quality of power. One can possess institutionalized rank and power, but power is never finally or ultimately acquired, but is contested, vied for and negotiated throughout an interaction. The analysis of the data in the study shows that certain discourse actions which have been traditionally seen as dominant or powerful behavior (cf. Zimmerman and West, 1975; Davis, 1988), such as introducing a topic, bidding for and getting the floor, and even interrupting others, require the validation and ratification of other actors. This work will show that there is an inherent insecurity in the task of vying for power. Bidding for the floor, competing with other participants for the floor and for a turn at talk, or trying to get one's ideas across are actions which require acknowledgment and ratification from other participants in the form of appropriate responses, answers, or even permission. Being powerful or leading a meeting are images of one's self (cf. Goffman, 1967) which are communicated to other actors; they need to be perceived by others present. In this sense, they are performances. Thus, power or leadership are actors' self images which are presented to other participants, and require ratification and acknowledgment. Power is not only a commodity which can be taken by force, but also a role which needs ratification.

This observation leads us to a *consensual* view of power; power is shared by all participants in an interaction. Because an actor needs his or her self-image to be ratified, those in the position to ratify it hold power in that they may withhold their ratification and acknowledgment, thus denying someone the successful attainment of leadership or power. Political effectiveness, therefore, expresses more adequately the dynamic quality of power, in particular the politic behavior necessary for contesting and negotiating the roles and self images in a relationship. Studies of power have consistently overlooked this consensual aspect to power. Power is often equated with status, and believed to be located in the individual of higher institutional rank in a given interaction. For instance, the institutionalized rank invested in professionals such as doctors, therapists and teachers has been automatically equated with power (cf. Davis, 1988; Lakoff, 1989). One need only look carefully at these interactions, however, to see that even in such cases, power can still be contested. The conversational data from discourse between doctors and patients show that the "inferior" person has strategies and ploys at his or her disposal to thwart the power of a status superior, as any therapist, teacher or policeman can attest.[6] Consensual power is close to Foucault's understanding of power as

> something which circulates ... It is never localised here or there, never in anybody's hands, never appropriated as a commodity or piece of wealth. Power is

---

[6] It would be well worth studying power as a social variable in flux, one that all participants in all situations can exercise. One might want to discover, for instance, how power is exercised by those in typically "weaker" positions: prisoners, patients, students, workers.

employed and exercised through a net-like organization. And not only do individuals circulate its thread, they are always in the position of simultaneously undergoing and exercising this power. They are not only its inert or consenting target; they are always also the elements of its articulation. In other words, individuals are the vehicles of power, not its points of application (1980:98).

Thus, power is political and consensual. It is the ability to interpret the events and issues of a time and place, and have these interpretations accepted. It is not only a property invested in an individual or a status, but a self-image or role which is contested, vied for and negotiated in discourse, and which needs ratification from others. There is thus no one person who is said to be in sole possession of power; likewise, there cannot be one person who is said to be solely powerless or weak.

## 1.4. Conversation and interpersonal meaning

The central idea behind such a study is that language is not only used to convey information, but, as an interactional device, can also shed light on interpersonal meanings and social relations. As Brown and Yule state,

[t]hat function which language serves in the expression of "content" we will describe as transactional, and that function involved in expressing social relations and personal attitudes we will describe as interactional (1983:1).

These personal attitudes and social relations are communicated in many ways by speakers: by what people say, by how they say it, by the types of utterances speakers make, by the conversational structure, by the tone of voice, and by the way turns at talk are distributed among participants. This work is undertaken very much in the spirit of Labov and Fanshel, who found, while attempting to transcribe intonation in discourse, that,

the lack of clarity or discreteness in the intonational signals is not an unfortunate limitation of this channel but an essential and important aspect of it. Speakers need a form of communication which is deniable. It is advantageous for them to express hostility, challenge the competence of others, or express friendliness and affection in a way that can be denied if they are explicitly held to account for it. If there were not such a deniable channel of communication...then some other mode of deniable communication would undoubtedly develop (1977:46).

This "hidden" or "deniable" level of language containing social, relational and emotional information about the speakers and the larger context constitutes the web which connects the speakers to each other and hence reveals the social structure of the group.

The way in which the members of the organization talk to one another in large groups, small groups, meetings, parties, and casual exchanges illustrates the social relationships and structure of the organization. The choices of talk that people make at all levels are of value here. It is of interest to us to know not only which topics may be raised in this group, but also how they are raised, by whom, when, and in what way. How do the members communicate with each other? What is the interactional quality of this community? Do people disagree with each other? How are disagreements and conflicts managed? Does the way an individual manages conflict reflect his or her social status within the organization? In observing the free verbal interaction of a group of people, whether they be two people, a family, a hospital staff, a classroom, the faculty of a university, or an urban street gang, one finds that the hierarchies, members' statuses, and power differentials are communicated through talk. The roles the members take, whether leadership or follower roles, the relative security of the members, the newcomers, the "insiders" and the "outsiders," the group taboos as well as the group's ideology is social information revealed in the members' conversations.

## 2. The dynamics of social activity

Maintaining the equilibrium of a social interaction means that the individual participants must continually see to it that, while power is contested, the entire system of relationships remains intact. Individuals, in their contacts with others, are, on the one hand, engaged in establishing, maintaining and furthering their positions in the group, and on the other hand, ensuring that the group, as well as their membership in it, remain intact. Within any interaction, interpersonal roles are assigned, rejected, disputed and negotiated. For example, whoever has the floor can be said, at that moment, to be the leader or central point of the interaction. The role of the speaker, in Western European/North American cultures, is one that is usually contested among members. When participants are raising topics, trying to get the floor, interrupting each other, and fending off interruptions, they are competing with each other for the position of central resource person, and by so doing, are furthering their local rank, their position in the group. Furthering one's position, however, must not jeopardize the group or the individual's membership in it. There is thus a built-in barrier against going too far. When the threshold is crossed, interpersonal relationships threaten to break down. These dynamics of interpersonal communication, i.e. the assertion and negotiation of individual status and the maintenance and strengthening of group bonds, can be considered constraints on social interaction.

These constraints ensure that social interaction proceeds in an orderly and coherent fashion. Most social interaction does. In fact, we tend to become aware of our social interactions only at those moments when the constraints fail, or threaten to do so. When a social interaction is marked by embarrassment, when interactants display behavior which clearly stands outside of social norms, and when moments of tension and conflict arise, we can speak of an interaction which does not adhere to social constraints. Erving Goffman (1967) has discussed these constraints in terms of presenting a positive self-image and the maintenance of face in face-to-face interaction. Social interaction and behavior works because "...the person tends to conduct himself during an encounter so as to maintain both his own face and the face of the participants (Goffman, 1967:11). By "face" Goffman means "the positive social value a person effectively claims for himself...during a particular contact. Face is an image of self delineated in terms of approved social attributes..."(1967:5). The constraints which surround contact are apparent in the individual's ritual behavior, as seen in public behavior, greetings, farewells, etc. which maintain and protect an individual's positive self-image, and maintain and protect the others' self images as well.

It is more than mere coincidence that speakers manage to understand each other, that conversation proceeds in a coherent, orderly and understandable fashion, where participants take turns speaking, make relevant contributions, ask questions, give pertinent replies, manage interruptions, avoid conflict where possible, and where not possible, negotiate it when it arises. As Goffman states,

[m]uch of the activity occurring during an encounter can be understood as an effort on everyone's part to get through the occasion and all the unanticipated and

unintentional events that can cast participants in an undesirable light, without disrupting the relationships of the participants. And if the relationships are in the process of change, the object will be to bring the encounter to a satisfactory close without altering the expected course of the development (1967:41).

Preserving the homeostasis during social encounters and maintaining one's positive face to the other interactants is accomplished through the vehicle of social activity: talk. When people talk, they communicate more than just information; they communicate images of themselves that they want others to accept, and they communicate their definitions of the relationship they are engaged in. They are, in point of fact, defining themselves, defining the relationship, and thus defining their conversational partners.

Presenting a positive self-image is a contextually dependent activity. The self-image that we effectively claim for ourselves in interaction is an image which is meaningful within the context of the interaction, within the set of socially acceptable self-images of a given group. Presenting a positive self-image depends on the other interactant's ability to receive or acknowledge our claim. Self-images may not be received because of a number of different factors. We may fail in successfully communicating the self-image. The self-image may be rejected or ignored by other interactants because it is deemed socially unacceptable. One reason why our self-images may be refused is that it is threatening to the other interactants, for defining oneself defines the others engaged in interaction. For example, if person A presents himself or herself to B as a peer or fellow student, this necessarily defines B as an equal. It could also be that A presents himself or herself as a teacher, superior or skilled professional, for example, thus defining B as a student, inferior or novice. Thus, the most basic aspect of interaction, presentation of positive self-image, happens against a backdrop of latent conflict surrounding these *de facto* definitions. The conversation, therefore, becomes a careful negotiation and management of this backdrop of conflict.

The presentation of a positive self-image takes different forms in different cultures. In particular, White European/American culture prescribes a positive self-image of individualism. The individual seeks to stand out and shine against the backdrop of the group. Folk expressions attest to this; compliments include, "He's a real individual," "She really stands out," "He's his own man," etc. Pejorative terms include "sheep," "follower," "can't think for himself," "a yes-man" or "ass-kisser." Standing out from the group may take the verbal form of getting and holding the floor, leading a meeting, vetoing others' suggestions, interrupting or successfully fending off others' interruptions. The overriding social need of presenting a positive self-image, whether it entails standing out and aggressive self assertion, or blending in, acquiescence and submission to the social order, is a dynamic flux that depends upon the context of the interaction and its participants. Self-image, in certain contexts, is best maintained through distance, whereas in other contexts, it is best maintained through intimacy. As Goffman states, "[b]etween status equals we may expect to find interaction guided by symmetrical familiarity" (1967:64). Between people of different status, however, there is more ceremonial distance, as seen in terms of address, physical distance, etc. The kind of group one is in determines the type of positive self-image and the way one projects it.

In all social organizations and interactions, from a momentary dyadic exchange, to a board of directors' meeting, to a family dinner time chat, we can witness the dynamic of, on the one hand, the individual asserting the self over the group, and, on the other hand, the need to preserve and strengthen the unity of the group, thus overriding the needs of the individuals. As Tannen states,

> [h]uman relationships become a matter of juggling the need for involvement with other people and the need to be independent; in other words, we juggle the need for and the danger of being close (1984:2).

Goffman (1959) discusses this point at length in noting that people not only present positive self-images, and desire these to be maintained, appreciated and acknowledged, but at the same time require a degree of social distance, separateness and avoidance. He quotes Durkheim, who says that

> [t]he human personality is a sacred thing; one does not violate it nor infringe its bounds while at the same time the greatest good is in communion with others (1953:37).

## 2.1. Politeness and social relationships

Brown and Levinson (1978, 1987) discuss this dual dynamic of closeness or solidarity on the one hand, and avoidance and deference on the other. In short, the authors, using Goffman's notion of face, maintain that the individual is motivated by the need to satisfy his or her positive or negative face wants. Positive face is the need to present oneself positively, to be liked, to be seen as friendly. It is "the want of every member that his wants be desirable to at least some others" (Brown and Levinson, 1978:67). Positive face want is the need to be seen as peer or equal; it is the necessity to establish a bond with the other. Negative face wants are the wants not to impose and not to be imposed upon. Deference and avoidance in polite language usage are strategies which satisfy negative face wants. Brown and Levinson show the strategies participants use to satisfy both the need to look good in the eyes of others, and the need not to impose on the other and not to be imposed upon.

In this study, politeness is one way in which social relationships are enacted. The various strategies of polite language usage are tools for the managing of interpersonal relationships. They become subsets of the larger notion of what Watts (1989) calls *politic linguistic behavior*. Watts maintains that the goal of discourse is not so much the maintaining of the individual's face through polite usage, but rather the maintaining of the entire fabric of interpersonal relationships. He defines politic linguistic behavior as

> socio-culturally determined behavior directed towards the goal of establishing and/or maintaining in a state of equilibrium the personal relationships between the individuals of a social group, whether open or closed, during the ongoing process of interaction. Any imbalance in the structure of such interdependent relationships may lead to a disturbance in the interaction and a possible breakdown of communication (1989:135).

Thus, politeness is only one strategy of politic linguistic behavior, which can be defined as a form of relational work, the task of continually negotiating and maintaining the relationships in the group. As we shall see in the members' interactions, relationship is a continual negotiation, balancing forces which threaten to dissolve the system and forces which strive to maintain its homeostasis.

## 3. Data collection and methodology

### 3.1. The community under observation

The cultural context in this study is a sub-group or sub-culture. It is one group of people within a city defined by their profession and their general interests. They are a group of students and practitioners of psychotherapy, members of a newly formed and still developing training institute for psychotherapy. The institute consists of three main groups: the trainers, who are, for the most part, founders of the institute; the trainees, who vary quite considerably in their age and professional background; and the wider body of members, associates and participants who sporadically attend meetings, classes and lectures. This study focuses on a subgroup of trainers and trainees, a tight-knit group with mutual and multipurpose relationships. Some of the members have known each other for over ten years. The members frequently overlap in their points of contact; they see each other for professional, social and business reasons, and often meet and interact in different capacities and roles. Thus, the group shares a psychological ideology, assumptions, goals and background. We will use a network analysis in order to highlight certain features of this speech community. A network study, as we shall see in the next chapter, brings to light the patterns of social interaction and communication in a speech community. It also illustrates the salient internal social features of the community which are necessary to make sense of many of the interactions between participants.

### 3.2. Suitability for the study

Factors that contribute to the suitability for the study concern the structure of the organization. The organization's hierarchy is not formally legitimized, but exists informally. The community is based on an egalitarian ideology which promotes equality between trainers and students and which discourages hierarchical decision making. Because decision making and rank is not rigidly fixed through hierarchy, and minimal social distance between members exists, individuals vie for rank more overtly, and individual authority and power is often contested through discourse. The data show us how members frequently contest

rank, power and relationship through conversation, using interaction
devices such as interruptions, bidding for and holding the floor,
argument, etc. Finally, the community is an ideal one in which to gather
and record data, for there are many meetings that are open to all trainers
and trainees in which organizational-level decisions are decided. The
decisions are arrived at through group consensus, rather than by rule,
voting or authority. These non-mediated, open discussions were an ideal
setting for gathering free verbal discourse between members of varying
statuses.

## 3.3. The recordings of the speech situations

The data are approximately 25 hours of recorded conversation from
members of a training organization for psychotherapy in Zurich,
Switzerland. The speakers are primarily American and Swiss German.
Swiss German is a collective term for over thirty mutually
comprehensible Alemmanic dialects of German spoken in the German
part of Switzerland, which reveals a diglossic[7] language situation: two
distinct linguistic codes, sufficiently distinct for the layman to call
separate languages, with one (high German) used on formal and public
occasions and the other (Swiss German) used by everybody in everyday
circumstances (Hudson, 1980:54). The Swiss German spoken in this
community is the Zurich German variety. Given the bilingual nature of
the institute, the choice of language provides us with information about
the members' relationships.[8]

Most of the members of the group can be considered bilingual. As
Romaine (1989) points out, bilingualism is difficult to define because
"the point at which the speaker of a second language becomes bilingual is
either arbitrary or impossible to determine." Following Mackey
(1968:555), Romaine comes to define bilingualism as the "alternate use
of two or more languages." Most of the members of the institute do have

---

[7]    cf. Ferguson, 1959.
[8]    At the time the research was carried out (1986-1988) the members of the institute
were primarily North American and Swiss. Since then, the institute has gone through
changes of locale, membership and structure, resulting in an increase of members
from different countries. It would be noteworthy to document the changes in language
and the effects that the multinational membership has on the English spoken among
members.

alternate use of both the Zurich dialect and some variety of English. Romaine acknowledges that the bilingual's skill may not be the same for both languages, but can differ at the lexical, syntactic, stylistic, phonological and semantic levels. For example, one Swiss German speaker has an excellent command of English vocabulary and grammar, but speaks with a heavy Swiss accent; his degree of bilingualism at the phonological level is significantly lower than his degree of bilingualism at the syntactic and semantic levels.

In situations such as this, where speakers have a choice of language or code,[9] it has been observed (Gumperz,1972, 1974, 1977; Blom & Gumperz, 1972; Heller, 1988) that the choice of code reflects social information about the participants, in particular their social role, status, and the social network and its boundaries. For example, one code may be used to signal in-group or out-group standards. As Gumperz (1982) says, "[i]t is this overtly marked separation between in- and out-group standards which perhaps best characterizes the bilingual experience" (1982:65). In the organization under observation bidialectalism is a marker of high prestige since it is (particularly for Americans and non-Swiss) directly proportionate to the length of involvement in the organization, and hence marks the degree of belonging.

While most social and official contacts are conducted in Swiss German or English, often a mix of languages arises. It has often been the case that newcomers to the group or visitors from outside notice the degree of code switching, language interference, accommodation and borrowings. In fact, the effect that the cooperation between the Swiss and Americans has had on the language would in itself warrant a study of microscopic language contact situations, such as that in areas of commerce, business and professional purposes, as opposed to macroscopic situations of countries, ethnic groups and political versus ethnic borders. For the purpose of this study, however, I am chiefly concerned with the ways in which codes are used to signal social meanings.

---

[9]   The term "code" is preferred to the term language. The reason for this is, as Hymes says, "[e]ven where there is but a single "language" present in a community (no cases are known in the contemporary world), that language will be organized into various forms of speech" (Hymes, 1972:63).

The trainers and trainees in the study consist of a group of about 20 people. They were recorded over two years, 1986-1988, during meetings, discussions and informal social gatherings. The recordings were carried out with the group's knowledge and permission, with the goal of gathering as many different speech situations and events as possible. Approximately 25 hours of conversation were recorded, but due to quality of recording, only 17 hours of conversation were usable. The speech situations recorded were casual exchanges, dinner parties, business meetings, administrative meetings, faculty meetings, general assemblies and executive committee meetings. Of the 17 usable hours of conversation, 11 hours were transcribed and used in this study. The criteria for choosing the 11 hours were the auditory quality of recording and the relative ease of transcribing the tapes. Some tapes were simply inaudible due to background noises or the poor quality of the tape recorder. Other tapes were unusable because there were too many simultaneous conversations happening, or because there were too many people present to recognize individual voices. The speech situations are as follows:

**TR01**

*Situation:* Faculty meeting.

*Topic:* Curriculum for an up-coming conference with international participation.

*Speech Event:* Activity centered, leaderless discussion.

*Participants:* 20 faculty members of different statuses (senior teachers, new teachers, assistants); mixed speakers of American English (AE) and Zurich dialect (ZG).

**TR02**

*Situation:* Administrative meeting of conference organizers over dinner at a restaurant.

*Topic:* Organizing a party; setting a date.

*Speech Event:* Activity centered, leaderless discussion.

*Participants:* 4 women, peers and friends; 3 native speakers of AE, 1 native speaker of ZG.

**TR03**

*Situation:* Thanksgiving dinner.

*Topic:* Parents' visits to Zurich.
*Speech Event:* Dinner time chat.
*Participants:* 7 friends of mixed status; all native AE speakers.

## TR04

*Situation:* Faculty meeting.
*Topic:* Evaluation forms from the conference.
*Speech Event:* Activity centered discussion with a leader.
*Participants:* 20 faculty members of different status, meeting led by institute president and founder. Mixed speakers of AE and ZG.

## TR05

*Situation:* Administrative meeting for the conference, over dinner at someone's home.
*Topic:* Scholarships, room and board costs.
*Speech Event:* Activity centered, leaderless discussion
*Participants:* 3 friends and peers; native AE speakers.

## TR06

*Situation:* Dinner time chat at someone's home.
*Topic:* Food likes and dislikes; taping the conversation; a request for a ride.
*Speech Event:* Informal chat.
*Participants:* 3 native AE speakers. 2 are long time friends and peers. The third is a newcomer, and a newcomer to the other two's home.

## 4. Conclusion

The next chapter, "Language in Context," is an overview of linguistics as applied to the social context. In particular, discourse analysis, sociolinguistic theories and network studies will be reviewed, including roles, power and status, and how these concepts are used here. A detailed presentation of the community's network structure, the ranking of members and their interrelationships will be given. Chapters 3, 4 and 5 take a closer look at the talk of this community: how speakers use strategies for signaling meaning within social relationships. As in all fields which study human behavior, rules of human behavior become visible when they are broken. The rules of linguistic behavior and interaction are most easily discernible where the smooth functioning threatens to break down. Thus, in these chapters the focus is on the breaks in continuity, areas of conflict, and mismanagement of the discourse which highlight strategies for management, repair and negotiation. Interactions in which conflict is implicit or explicit and where the speaker must navigate between the opposing needs of self-image and group identity will be shown. Chapter 6 concludes the study with a discussion of its implications for the structure of interpersonal relationships, the dynamic between individual status and group preservation, power as consensual, conflict and competition in discourse, and strategies for the management of interpersonal relationships through discourse.

# Chapter Two: Language in a Social Context

## 1. Language in use

Studies of language in use are concerned with the social matrix in which language is embedded. Discourse features and variations in language use only take on meaning within the larger social context in which the variations occur. As the study of language in its social context has a long and varied tradition, discussing it in its entirety would fall outside of the scope of this study. I shall therefore limit the discussion to a broad overview of studies of language in context that bear direct relevance to this study. After reviewing traditional sociolinguistics and language and speech communities, we will turn to the study of networks, and their application to discourse analysis and speech communities. Finally we will examine the network of the community under study, the linguistic and social variables at work within it, and the relationship between network, social variables, rank and power.

### 1.1. Sociolinguistics: from field linguistics to social class

The analysis of language in its natural setting brought the linguist into the field. Field linguistics has its antecedents in nineteenth century anthropological linguistics and dialectology. American anthropologists and linguists such as Franz Boas, Benjamin Lee Whorf and Edward Sapir recorded the language of Native American informants in the hopes of expanding the corpus of known languages and cultures. Their methodology, however, using an informer-elicitor technique, had some drawbacks. For one, the phonetic and cultural system of the elicitor imposed restrictions on the data gathered. The transcriptions of phonemes could only be done with a degree of interference from the fieldworker's own phonetic system. Also, syntactic, semantic, and even pragmatic biases of the fieldworkers were imposed upon the data collected. Another drawback to the informant-elicitor model was that utterances were recorded independent of an authentic speech situation.

Thus, the language was not "living," but constructed according to the fieldworker's questions.

The second approach to language in the field was dialectology, dating back to the nineteenth century. The dialectologist attempted to document language change, linking contemporary forms to earlier ones, and thus proving that sound changes are regular and describable in terms of rules. Studying chiefly phonological and lexical variation along geographical and regional lines, variations in dialect among the population were charted. Differences in dialect were seen as functions of regional variation. Differences in individual speakers and within one speech community were studiously avoided by using older men as informants whenever possible because it was thought that younger speakers and city dwellers were more subject to influences from the contact with speakers from other regions, cultures and countries. The speech situation, too, was not taken into consideration. All social or individual factors resulting in variability were systematically excluded from the study. Labov's (1966, 1972a, 1972b) pioneering work of locating language change in real time used methods which extended the concept of linguistic variation to include differences of speaker and of speech situation. Labov attempted to see language change in progress by studying language variation in Martha's Vineyard and New York City. Rather than avoid the seemingly chaotic variations of language, Labov sought to find regularities governing when, where and how they occurred. He found that the variable of social class was one factor in language variation.

By correlating linguistic variables with social features of socio-economic class, ethnicity, age and sex, Labov brought the linguist deeper into the social matrix. Labov was interested in how linguistic variables co-vary with extra-linguistic, independent variables such as social class, age, sex, ethnic group or contextual style (L. Milroy, 1980:10). His study, originally intended to discover the motivation for language change, revealed differences in the speech communities between speech situations, men and women, and social classes. Labov was one of the first to show that speakers use language as a marker of social features, such as ethnic identification, group membership, age, sex, etc. He also broke new ground by considering the different types of speech situations and the speech communities under study: their history, population, demography, etc. As Blom and Gumperz (1972) point out in their study of code switching in a Norwegian community, the linguist studying language use within a speech community should have a thorough knowledge and understanding of the norms and values of the community before interpreting the linguistic data. This element changed pure linguistic fieldwork into ethnographic documentation.

A linguistic variable is a useful tool only within the definitions of the community in which it appears. Labov found social class a useful concept within the New York City study, but it did not illuminate the variations among the phonemes he researched on Martha's Vineyard. Instead, he found that the distinctions between islander and non-islander, or local and tourist, correlated with the linguistic variables under observation. This finding has been confirmed in other studies, most notably those within the lower and working class communities where variables were used by speakers as a way of showing "in-group" or "local-team" loyalty. The variable of social class as Labov used it in his study of sound change in New York City (1966) was actually a variable of socio-economic class, occupation, education and income. Yet once again, as the dialectologists found with the variable of region, it was insufficient to correlate linguistic variables with social variables of region or socio-economic class alone. Within any one social class, for instance, there are numerous subcultures that demonstrate linguistic forms at a variance with others of their social class. Labov (1966), J. Milroy (1981) and Milroy and Milroy (1985) found, for instance, that within a particular social class there are variations between men and women, and between older and younger speakers. As J. Milroy states about his study of Belfast English,

> within working class speech alone,...research has demonstrated that there are considerable differences between individuals, between different speech-styles, between men and women, and between older and younger speakers (1981: 89).

Like region, social class as a variable might reveal no noticeable differentiation when researching language use among other kinds speech communities. For example, linguistic diversity among school children, institutions, the work place, a neighborhood, a circle of friends, a college or university, or even a branch of the armed forces cannot be attributable solely to social class difference. In fact, it is difficult to imagine one social variable, whether social class, age, ethnicity or sex, that could be a determining factor across all social groups. Each speech community has its own internally significant linguistic variable that co-varies with social factors.

## 1.2. The ethnography of speaking

In keeping with these factors, Gumperz (1964, 1972b, 1982), Hymes (1962, 1972) Gumperz and Hymes (1964, 1972) and Blom and Gumperz (1972) take a different approach in their work on language and social context. These authors argue that social variables alone cannot account for the profusion of linguistic diversity, and that linguistic diversity is much more than the variance of phonemes. Speakers, they maintain, have a variety of codes or repertoires at their disposal, and know when and in which situation to use which repertoire. For example, when talking casually to friends at a bar, a student would use a very different repertoire than when talking to a professor in a lecture. These differences of repertoires are encoded phonetically, syntactically and lexically. To account for linguistic diversity, therefore, one must look to the immediate environment in addition to the wider social environment. Situational factors include the type of activity: a party, business meeting, church service, or train ride. Each situation contains speech events specific to it: for example, small talk at a cocktail party, discussions at business meetings, sermons at church services, and chats on a train. It is necessary to take into consideration context, setting and participants to make an interpretation of the speakers' linguistic choices. Speakers deliberately manipulate the variables of codes and situations to create social meanings.

Gumperz gives an excellent example of how a speaker signals meaning by using one code in a situation which calls for another:

Following an informal graduate seminar at a major university, a black student approached the instructor, who was about to leave the room accompanied by several other black and white students, and said,

Student: Could I talk to you for a minute? I'm gonna apply for a fellowship and I was wondering if I could get a recommendation?

Instructor: O.K. Come along to the office and tell me what you want to do.

As the instructor and the rest of the group left the room, the black student said, turning his head ever so slightly to the other students:

Student: Ahma git me a gig! (Rough gloss: "I'm going to get myself some support.") (1982:30)

The student switched into Black English where Standard English was called for, i.e. in a classroom at a university. Gumperz gave this example to a number of different students and asked them what they thought happened. All of the judges "treated [the] inquiries as calling for interpretation of intent...". One group of judges, all of them black except for one, interpreted this switch of codes as a signal that the black was "still in control," that is, by indicating to his friends that he was just "playing the white person's game" to get what he wanted.

This approach to linguistic diversity can be said to be ethnographic in that what is transcribed by the observer is not just the linguistic utterance, but the entire culture in which the utterance is embedded. Choices in repertoire are interpreted within the context. The speaker's ability to produce and comprehend meaningful utterances within context and to choose among different repertoires reflects a knowledge of not only language, but of communication skills. Speakers have communicative competence, not just language competence, for speaking a language means speaking it within a certain context, at a certain time, to certain people, and from a range of possible repertoires. Speakers are able to choose from their repertoires to create meanings in different situations and to navigate within the rules of social discourse. The ability to vary speech depending on context and situation is a speaker's communicative competence.

If speakers create meanings in their choice of repertoires, this depends on other speakers having knowledge of that repertoire as well. Speakers belong to a number of different speech communities, and vary their speech according to context. Choosing among alternative modes of speaking, depending on context and situation, signals social meaning, as long as speakers have knowledge of the different repertoires available. In order for a speaker to decode the meaning of a particular language variant,

[a]ll that is required is that there be at least one language in common and that rules governing basic communicative strategies be shared so that speakers can decode the social meanings carried by alternative modes of communication (Gumperz, 1972b:16).

Blom and Gumperz speak of "metaphorical switching," the use of code switching to signal a social meaning, usually an "in-group" or "local-team" identification. The same has been found in the inner city, where use of the vernacular, in contrast to the standard, is a strong signal of belonging to the tight knit local community.

The concept of community differs from that of social class in that the latter groups speakers according to factors with which they themselves might not necessarily identify. Community, on the other hand, both community in the mind and community on the ground, groups speakers according to factors that have psychological reality for them. It is a function of a specific time and place, and the speakers can assign membership to themselves and to others within the speech community. This is not to invalidate the concept of social class. Many linguistic variables correlate with social class factors. Yet, in some cases, social class distinctions do not correspond with the speaker's own social identity. Class also does not necessarily reflect the communication patterns. If language change and variation are dependent upon language use, then the social unit one correlates with the linguistic variables must reflect the patterns of language use. It is pointless to speak of any social unit that does not correspond to a speaker's language usage, and to that speaker's own notions of the community to which she or he belongs. In other words, language spreads along lines of communication usage or networks.

## 2. Social networks

The social network has come into prominence as a means of mapping kinship and friendship ties in urban and rural areas. It was first used by Barnes (1954) to describe how individuals used personal ties of kinship and friendship in Bremnes, Norway. Bott (1957) also used networks in her studies of families in London. The term came into usage partly as a reaction against the structural-functionalist school of sociology which had been dealing increasingly with systems and structures, and less with the people populating the systems. Network analysis brought the person back into sociological research (cf. Boissevain, 1974). A network is a methodological tool to describe people's contacts within a community or group. More specifically, it charts the various kinds of ties an individual has to others. A tie may be communication, services or goods exchanged. Networks can chart a single individual's contacts within a group, which is an ego-centric model of relationship, or they can depict the contact between members in an entire group or community. Networks also portray the intensity of contact between members (density), the kinds of contact between members (multiplexity), and areas of particular density within the network (clustering).

A network is a useful tool in language studies for it describes the social communication pattern, the natural lines of communication a speaker creates. These may or may not reflect the larger social units of social class, sex, ethnic or religious affiliation, etc. Furthermore, within one social network, certain social factors might correlate with the linguistic variation and lines of communication. In linguistic studies of urban areas (Labov, 1972; L. Milroy, 1980; J. Milroy 1981; Milroy and Milroy, 1985), it has been found that the network of social contacts resembles the close knit ties of village or family patterns. There is a strong sense of territory in the inner cities, and an equally strong sense of belonging; outsiders are recognized immediately and treated as such. Milroy and Milroy describe that in their

research, it has become evident that the concept of "network" is of the greatest importance in interpreting results (Bott, 1957; Boissevain, 1974). Like core working-class areas in other large cities...the Belfast communities are characterized by dense overlapping kin and friendship networks...These dense close-knit networks are maintained by a number of mechanisms such as extended visiting, corner-hanging, and (most important of all) a homogeneous traditional form of employment located within the area (1985: 23).

Network studies complement the notion of speech community. If we want to find the community to which a speaker belongs, we would need to find the patterns of contact and of communication which the speaker creates in his or her interactions. By finding out who talks to whom and how much, we can determine to which and how many speech communities the speaker belongs.

## 2.1. Network density

Boissevain defines network density as

the degree to which the members of a person's network are in touch with each other independently of him...That is, 'the extent to which links which could possibly exist among persons do in fact exist' (1974:37).

In other words, network density is the percentage of actual namings to the number of possible namings. Boissevain's model of network is an egocentric one. The network is a measurement of one person's contacts with others. It depicts an individual's contact, as opposed to the members' contacts with each other. Boissevain depicts all namings, contrasted with the number of possible namings.

Where speakers interact within a specific territory such as a neighborhood in the inner city, the contact between them is said to be one of high density. Examples of high density networks are people who live in the same neighborhood, work at the same factory, whose children go to the same school, and who get together socially. In lower working class and inner city neighborhoods there is more opportunity for overlapping contacts: houses are built closer together or people live in apartment buildings, there are neighborhood schools, and there is a tendency for men and women to find work locally. In addition, there is a good deal of social activity in the neighborhood. Groups of children play on the streets, teenagers frequent certain stores or street corners, and adults visit each other frequently and informally. A low density network, on the other hand, is one in which the contacts are generally restricted to one social domain, as for example in the urban middle class, or suburban middle to upper middle classes. In the suburbs personal contacts are spread out, not necessarily located in a certain physical locality, and generally not overlapping in more than one domain. Some contacts are from the family, others from the job, some from the neighborhood. It is rather the exception that neighbors are also working colleagues. The contacts themselves also rarely overlap, that is, an individual's contacts do not frequently have contact with each other.

## 2.2. Network multiplexity

A multiplex network is one in which each individual is connected to another through multiple ties, or strands, not just one (Boissevain, 1974). For example, if John is Mary's colleague, but they are also on the same bowling team, they are said to have a multiplex network relationship.

They would name each other as contacts in regard to at least two different roles. It has been noted elsewhere (Bernstein, 1971; L. Milroy, 1980) that network multiplexity is a feature of closed, dense networks, such as those found in urban centers, working class neighborhoods and ghettos.

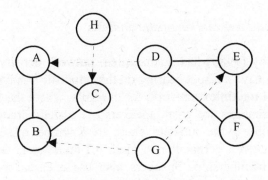

*Figure 2.1. Multiplex and Uniplex Ties*

The network in Figure 2.1 depicts multiplex ties as solid lines, and uniplex ties as dotted lines. The individuals linked through multiplex ties (A, B and C; D, E and F) form extremely dense parts of the network, called clusters.

## 2.3. Clusters

According to Boissevain, clusters are

segments or compartments of networks which have a relatively high density. The persons forming clusters are relatively speaking more closely linked to each other than they are with the rest of the network (1974: 43).

Clusters not only reflect network density, they also reflect multiplex ties, resembling what are called colloquially "cliques", "groups" or "gangs." A cluster consists of a portion of a network in which the members share an identity or are linked through a common role or activity. In a factory, for example, a cluster could be those factory workers working a particular job or shift. It could be a sub-group linked by certain common social features such as age; or it could be a sub-group linked by an activity or role set, such as members of the factory softball team. In an institution such as a school, a cluster might consist of members of the same class or age group. It might consist of junior faculty members, or members of the school band. In our data, the members of the two clusters are linked by social features of age and sex, as well as by their position within the institute.

## 2.4. Network features and linguistic analysis

As L. Milroy (1980) has documented, network density, multiplexity and clustering have a direct bearing on the linguistic behavior of a group. In a dense and multiplex network, for example, where the frequency and number of exchanges are great, speakers use casual vernacular which is often inaccessible to the outsider. There are a number of reasons for this. Speakers use such a vernacular to mark off their "turf," so to speak, to signal group membership. Speakers also use a casual vernacular that reflects their shared knowledge. Abbreviations, slang words and jargon reflect intimacy, in that their meanings need not be explained among speakers.

In addition, where there is a dense and multiplex network, there is greater pressure exerted on the individual to adapt to the group norms. This can be seen as pressure to adjust to and maintain the vernacular. In his study of the Black English Vernacular (BEV) Labov (1972a) found that there was a direct correlation between core group members of a gang and their use of BEV. He found that lames, or boys who were outside of the gangs, and socially stigmatized, tended to use Standard English forms more than core group members. Furthermore, L. Milroy (1980:61) points out that "extreme density produces a homogeneity of norms and values." These three factors, use of casual vernacular, pressure to adopt the norm, and homogeneity of norms and values are all visible in the speaking styles of closed networks, including the institute under observation.

The features of density, multiplexity and clustering are interrelated in a number of ways. Multiplexity and density are conditions which often co-occur, and both increase the effectiveness of the network as a norm-enforcement mechanism (Milroy L., 1980:52). Dense, multiplex networks are identifiable through the members' use of "in-language," shared meanings, and reliance on extraverbal or background assumptions. In addition, dense and multiplex networks become a community or a social unit where there is generally an ideology linking the members, a "local-team" spirit, a strong sense of belonging, of territory, of insiders and outsiders. The ideology gives rise to an internal set of social factors that have meanings for the members and that are encoded linguistically.

## 2.5. Networks and codes

Bernstein's (1971) concept of elaborated and restricted codes as an attempt to account for the alternative varieties of speech among different classes brought to light the differences in speech codes between open and closed networks. He noticed that speakers within a closed and dense network used a restricted code, while members of an open network used a more elaborated code. His work, while implicitly tending towards a normative value for language use, has brought to light an important feature of closed system speech patterns. Bernstein found that members of the working and lower classes tended to use primarily a restricted code, and that members of the middle and upper classes used an elaborated code. What he terms an *elaborated code* is a sufficiently lexically and syntactically rich code whose meanings are not implicit, but explicit. A *restricted code*, on the other hand, relies on background knowledge, and signals information through non-lexical means, often prosodic. Text level devices such as intonation, code switching, anaphora, stress, etc., are used.

Bernstein has been criticized for implying a value judgment with the terms "restricted" and "elaborated." Nevertheless, his observation is of value to us here because a restricted code is a code for *any dense, closed network*, regardless of class. There is no reason to infer that one code is more desirable than another. As Labov (1972b) has shown with his work in the inner city, creativity in speech is a universal; no one language or code enables a greater degree of creativity and productivity than another. Also, dense networks within businesses, schools and institutions of various kinds use restricted codes. There is no reason to assume that the restricted code is limited to lower classes; its value lies in what it shows us about networks and groups. As Bernstein writes,

[a] restricted code will arise where the form of the social relation is based upon closely shared identifications, upon an extensive range of shared expectations, upon a range of common assumptions. ...Communication goes forward against a backcloth of closely shared identifications and affective empathy which removes the need to elaborate meanings and logical continuity in the organization of speech (1972: 476).

## 2.6. Networks and social variables

Social classifications, whether social class, sex, age or ethnic group, reflect an implicit, or, in some cases, explicit hierarchy in the social organization. It seems to be a characteristic of groups that they are segmented along a number of different parameters, and that the segments are often of a hierarchical nature. Thus, one group will be the identified prestige group, while another will be a stigmatized group. Note that these terms are not inherent properties of the groups themselves, but rather, social meanings which the members of the groups themselves identify. For a speech community where classifications such as social class fail to describe linguistic or social regularities, network classifications become meaningful. For example, in a dense and multiplex network, the concept of belonging, or degree of integration into the network is of primary importance. This concept can help classify members along lines of integration: insiders, outsiders, lames, etc. Integration into a network is the principle upon which the social classification of the network is based. We can define rank within a network in terms of integration. Those members who belong most securely to the network may be said to possess some measure of local rank within that network.

Naturally, there are factors that determine whether or not a member belongs. For a village network in rural Norway, belonging would be contingent upon region, i.e. whether the person lived there or not, and nativity, i.e. whether the person is a local or has moved there from somewhere else. Thus, a characteristic of many networks is length of involvement. In an inner city network, like the one Labov studied, certain activities that support the network ideology are determining characteristics. In the gangs that he studied, fighting and raising pigeons were the two activities central to the network. Those members who were the best fighters, and those who raised pigeons were likely to belong to the "inner core" of insiders. Insiders and outsiders are terms used to describe "belongingness." Thus, we see that rank, to a large extent, can be seen by the degree of belonging to or integration in the network, and carrying out those activities which support the group ideology and insure belongingness. As L. Milroy states, "[d]ensity, multiplexity and clustering can be used to measure an individual's degree of integration into local community networks" (1980:52). Group members' rank is related to the degree of network integration, and is attained by carrying out those activities, and displaying those characteristics which are enforced by the network. Degree of integration is not the only indication of rank, however. There may be other, outer and social factors operating. For example, in Labov's study of the Cobras and Jets, women and girls were excluded from the network. Thus, sex is a social factor which operates from the outside to determine network rank.

### 2.7. Networks and methodology

Networks can be depicted visually using a sociogram, a diagram showing the number and kinds of interconnections between members of a speech community (see figure 2.2, p.41). Sociograms depict the interconnections and amount of contact between members of a speech community, or they can be used to depict a social variable particular to the speech community in question. For example, in determining the status variables of the inner city gangs he researched, Labov used a sociographic description of the gang members' hang-out pattern. Labov was interested in the pattern of social organization and the degree of belonging to the core group. He differentiated core group members from "lames" or outsiders by asking the members questions to determine their degree of integration and how each member of the gang regarded the other members. Knowing that fighting skills carried status in the gang, Labov set out to measure status by asking the members to name the best fighters in the group. What is important to note about network surveys is that the social organization, degree of integration and ranking are group specific. In other words, each group has its own factors according to which members are ranked. A youth gang in the inner city would be ranked according to fighting skills, but a group of psychotherapists in an institute in Zurich, Switzerland, would not.

The use of networks has changed the methodology of field research. Instead of interviewing individual informants, the interviewer records and observes members of a group talking to one another. Thus, individuals are less likely to adapt their speech styles to the formality of the interview situation. In addition, group dynamics, which have direct bearing on linguistic style, are also apparent. A network has theoretical implications for research in the social sciences because it highlights language variation and group structure, not just individual language variation. A problem with the older method of social class or regional distinction was that it ran into the paradoxical problem of using the individual to account for a social feature. Many of the language variations that were under observation are variations that hold social meaning only within the group and not necessarily in isolation. Vernacular can be and is often adjusted depending upon the audience. Thus, using the network as a tool for our analysis will help us to understand the social context of the language used by the group. The social meanings in the vernacular can only be obtained by understanding the full social setting in which it occurs.

## 3. Network structure of the community

### 3.1. Overview of the community network

In understanding the interactions of the community members, it will be important for us to know both the institutional rank (age, nationality, gender, level of education) and the local rank (position within the organization) of the individuals involved. As we will see when we analyze verbal interactions, meanings become clearer when we know whether the interactants are trainers or trainees, close friends or distant acquaintances. Are they Swiss or American, of the same age and gender? Have they been involved in the organization for the same length of time? This information was gathered through a questionnaire[10] that was completed by a total of 27 members of the organization. Every participant recorded completed the questionnaire. The questionnaire sought to determine the following features of the organization: network

---

[10] The questionnaire can be found in the Appendix.

density, network sub-groups or clusters, and network multiplexity, or degree of contact between members. It also sought to determine relative institutional and local ranking of members, including their rank in organization as seen by other members, their length and degree of involvement in the organization, and their position in the organization (faculty, student). Also, external social variables were gathered, such as gender, nationality, mother tongue and degree of proficiency in second language. Some of these features are more relevant to the study than others. The questionnaire sought to cover as many of the organization's social features as possible.

## 3.2. Network density and multiplexity

Network density surveys the personal, social and professional contacts between members. Rather than use Boissevain's (1974) definition of network density, i.e. the number of namings of personal, social and professional contact between members, we measure network density by the number of reciprocal social contacts each member names. In addition, Boissevain measures network density as the number of namings compared to number of *possible* namings; again, this will not work as it is rare for members to name more than 4 or 5 people as close contacts. Using his measurements, 4 or 5 close social contacts out of a possible 27 would yield a low density measurement. For our purposes, it would be more useful to see network density as simply the number of reciprocal or mutual namings. Reciprocal namings are occurrences of two members naming each other as a social contact. If person X names person Y as an intimate friend, and person Y names person X as well, this would be reciprocity. The degree of in-group namings refers to the number of social contacts named by each individual that belong to the community. Some members' social contacts were mostly outside the institution while others were all members of the institute. Overall, the network is a very dense one. Only 6 out of 27 members, or 22% of the members have close social contact with people outside the institute. The rest, or 78%, have their primary social relationships with other members. Furthermore, many of the social contacts were reciprocal. The density also yields another feature within the network. The reciprocal namings result in clusters, or high density segments within the overall network. These clusters are like sub-groups within the larger organization. Dense subsections of the network, like cliques or sub-groups, exert a pressure to conform to group norms upon the members. Thus, we can expect to find particular styles of verbal interactions within and between clusters.

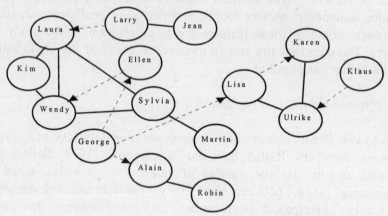

*Figure 2.2. Network Sociogram of the Institution*[11]

The contact between the members is also highly multiplex. Multiplex namings refer to the number of different domains that two contacts share, for instance two people who see each other socially may also belong to an organizational subgroup, the same training group, or a faculty group. Members were asked to describe the nature of the contact between themselves and others, that is, whether they saw each socially, professionally (as teacher, therapist, consultant), or administratively (as fellow committee members). Of the total namings between members, 85% of the time a member named at least one other member in at least two capacities or domains, as a social acquaintance, in a professional capacity as therapist, teacher, or supervisor, and in an administrative capacity. It is perhaps rare for a school to have such a multiplex network; this may reflect the fact that this is a newly formed and still developing institute with adult members, many of whom knew each other prior to joining the institute, and many of whom, both teachers and students, were instrumental in establishing the institute. Thus, many students and

---

[11]  Only those individuals who contribute to the recorded material appear in the sociogram.

teachers sit on administrative committees together, and have opportunity for social contact.

## 3.3. Ranking and status of members

The most important feature of the ranking of the members is that it is relative. Members are ranked according to features which are internally meaningful. Just as Labov asked gang members to indicate whom they considered the best fighters in the gang, the ranking of the members of this institution was conducted by asking internally significant questions. Moreover, many of the roles within this organization are not standardized or assigned. For instance, among faculty members, there is no established hierarchy of associate, assistant or full professor, like one finds at a university. Except for administrative positions, such as president, secretary, treasurer, etc., which satisfied the guidelines for a (Swiss) non-profit organization, there were no traditional positions within the training program designated for academic dean, dean of student affairs, director of training, etc. Thus, rank accorded through individuals' perceptions plays a large role in understanding the dynamics of social interaction.

Members were asked to evaluate others on the basis of activities meaningful to this institute: training, research, psychotherapy and administrative leadership. To determine local rank of members, participants were asked to name up to five members to whom they would go for a consultation about a difficult case. This question enabled the members to evaluate each others' therapeutic skills and simultaneously gave information on the multiplexity of the organization. Questionnaire participants were also asked to indicate which members served or have served as their therapists. Since personal therapy is a training requirement in this institute, as it is in many other psychotherapeutic training institutes, the choice of therapist becomes a meaningful variable in ranking. The trainee is able to choose freely among therapists. In addition to therapy and consultation, leadership is also a valued skill in this institute since it is based on a non-hierarchical model of organization. Those who are elected by others to sit on the executive committee, and those who take a leadership position are generally highly regarded by others. The members were asked to name up to five people under whose leadership they would feel secure. This question, however, yielded vague results as many people answered "anybody," and some of the senior members wrote down the names of the most recently joined members. This reflects the ideology of the institute, that leadership follows group consensus; the leader is only a role which must follow the general will of the people. Finally, members were asked to name whom they thought would be most likely to have a solution to a problem being discussed in a hypothetical meeting. This yielded clearer results than the preceding question. Finally, important to the ranking of members, participants were asked to state how long they were involved in the organization. Since this organization was founded not too long ago, many of the current trainers were among those who helped found it. Length of involvement is a good indication of rank.

## 3.4. Social variables

There are other, social variables which the questionnaire attempted to answer. Members were asked to name their mother tongue, their nationality, and also their degree of proficiency in their second language, either English or Swiss German. Degree of proficiency of second language, like length of involvement in the organization, is a prestige factor in the organization. For a participant to switch codes, or to follow a code switch of another participant, indicates length of involvement in the organization as well as degree of integration into both Swiss or English speaking cultures.

Lastly, members were asked to list their position in the organization and their academic degrees and qualifications. Position in the organization refers to whether participants are faculty members or trainees. Among the trainees, they can be advanced (diploma candidates, having passed their propaedeutika or theoretical exams) or beginners (pre-propraedeutika). Within the faculty, teachers are either "grandparents" (those awarded their status at the outset of the establishment of the institution; designated "GP" on Table 2.1) or diplomates (those who earned their status by graduating; designated "dipl." on Table 2.1). Grandparents are generally older, more experienced, and thus of higher rank than diplomates.

Institutional rank, that is, age, gender, nationality and length of time in the organization will be discussed in the following chapters, in the context of the interactions. Below is a list of the different members' institutional ranking, and local ranking, their rank relative to other members, based on members' perceptions. The local rank is based on the answers to the questions about therapeutic skill, leadership skill, and supervisory ability. It is the ratio of total number of times an individual was named to the number of possible namings.

*Table 2.1. Institutional and Local Rank of Community Members*

| Name * | Age | Gender | Length of Involvement | Nationality | Position | Local rank (% named by others) |
|---|---|---|---|---|---|---|
| Peter | 47 | Male | -- | US | Founder | 98.5% |
| Martin | 42 | Male | 15 yrs | Swiss | GP | 85% |
| Laura | 30 | Female | 7 yrs | US | Dipl | 59% |
| George | 42 | Male | 15 yrs | US | GP | 33% |
| Alain | 42 | Male | 10 yrs | Swiss | GP | 33% |
| Kim | 31 | Female | 7 yrs | US | Dipl | 22% |
| Wendy | 30 | Female | 7 yrs | US | Dipl | 22% |
| Ulrike | 44 | Female | 14 yrs | Swiss | GP | 20% |
| Sylvia | 30 | Female | 6 yrs | Swiss | Dipl | 16% |
| Klaus | 44 | Male | 11 yrs | Swiss | GP | 12% |
| Ellen | 29 | Female | 2 yrs | US | Student | 5% |
| Larry | 32 | Male | 3 yrs | US | Student | 5% |
| Lisa | 40 | Female | 15 yrs | US | GP | 4% |
| Robin | 30 | Female | 3 yrs | US | Student | 2.5% |
| Jean | 43 | Female | 5 yrs | US | Student | 1% |
| Karen | 40 | Female | 5 yrs | US | Dipl | 0% |

* The names of all the individuals in the institute have been changed. In the transcripts of the data, fictitious names for individuals, rather than initials or numbers are used for the reader's convenience

The institutional rank includes age, gender, nationality, position in the institution and length of involvement in the organization. The institution was formally founded in 1982. The formal training component was established in 1984. But the founder of the institute had been unofficially conducting training on his own since 1975. As the institution is centered around the philosophy and leadership of its founder and president, length of involvement will refer to the number of years each member has been associated with the founder as a trainee. Not all 27 members who received questionnaires are listed below, only those who have participated in the discussions, and are featured in the verbal discourse.

The next chapter is concerned with the organization of discourse and politic verbal behavior, that is, how individuals use talk to present positive self-images, assert and contest rank, and define their roles vis-a-vis each other, while preserving their relationship to others. We will be looking at sections of conversations between members of the community, specifically looking at how politic verbal strategies interface with the members' rank and position in the institution. Furthermore, by using the results of our network sociogram, we will see how discourse and politic verbal behavior reflect intercluster interaction and intracluster interaction.

# Chapter Three: Verbal Interaction:
# Balancing Individual and Group Wants

## 1. Introduction

In the last chapter we talked about methodologies of discourse analysis and analyzing verbal interaction *in situ*. In this chapter and the next we will analyze excerpts of multi-party interactions to find how members negotiate the need to present a positive self-image and the need to preserve the network to which they belong. This chapter introduces a general discussion of the ways social relationships and interpersonal dynamics can be discerned from discourse.

Interactions are not random, but highly patterned and predictable. In fact,

[i]t seems intuitively clear that any regularly interacting system such as a group of professionals, an adolescent peer group, a classroom, a family, or a courtroom will develop some internal regularities in its interaction patterns (Scollon and Scollon, 1981:175).

By analyzing the discourse of a group, we shall be able to see its specific patterns of interaction and come to understand its social relationships. After discussing strategies of discourse analysis, we will then investigate how participants navigate the need to present self-image without jeopardizing the social fabric of the community. Before looking at the interactions, we need to concern ourselves with some theoretical approaches to interaction. I shall briefly review models of verbal interaction which analyze the individual's negotiation of status and relationship. Goffman's concept of positive self-image and Brown and Levinson's model of social relationships and polite language usage will illustrate methods for interpreting the relationships and statuses underlying the data.

## 2. Self presentation and group preservation

Presenting a positive self-image can be defined as the individual's attempt to raise his or her rank in the eyes of others. It is similar to Goffman's concept of face, defined as

> an image of self delineated in terms of approved social attributes - albeit an image that others may share, as when a person makes a good showing for his profession or religion by making a good showing for himself (1967:5).

Brown and Levinson (1978), in their model of politeness in conversation, borrow Goffman's concept of face, but differentiate between

> (a) negative face: the basic claim to territories, personal preserves, rights to non-distraction- i.e., freedom of action and freedom from imposition, and (b) positive face: the positive consistent self-image or "personality" (crucially including the desire that this self-image be appreciated and approved of) claimed by interactants (1978: 66).

Face wants, for both Goffman and Brown and Levinson, are constraints that govern and motivate social interaction. In preserving, maintaining and enhancing face wants, interactants are acting in their own best interest, and ultimately in the best interest of the situation as well, for

> people cooperate in maintaining face in interaction, such cooperation being based on the mutual vulnerability of face. That is, normally everyone's face depends on everyone else's being maintained (Brown and Levinson, 1978:66).

What Brown and Levinson call politeness is a form of politic behavior (Watts, 1989): verbal interaction constrained by the need to maintain the entire network of social relationships, not just the individual's need to present a positive self-image. Scollon and Scollon (1981) have applied Brown and Levinson's model of face-work to analyze interethnic communication and relations between Athabaskan Indians and Americans in Alaska and northern Canada. The authors discuss negative and positive politeness in terms of solidarity and deference systems, respectively. They use these new terms to "characterize global systems of politeness." A solidarity system is one in which members

> favor the emphasis on sameness, of group membership, and the general good of the group. Deference politeness systems would favor deference, indirectness or even avoidance of making impositions on others (Scollon and Scollon, 1981:175).

Solidarity politeness furthers group membership and belonging; it is the language that addresses the "we" of a group. Deference politeness, on the other hand, maintains individual distance and boundaries. The way an individual presents his or her positive self-image or the politeness forms that an individual uses are specific to the social relationships in the group and the cultural context. For instance, solidarity politeness is most frequently used among status equals, while negative or deference politeness is used to maintain and respect status differences.

Whether we label it deference and solidarity or negative and positive politeness, speakers use a variety of strategies between two poles in interaction: self assertion and group preservation. The individual furthers his or her own rank at the expense of the others, and the individual furthers the group, its identity and his or her membership in it at the expense of his or her individual rank. Both tendencies are in the interest of the individual and thus can be seen as components of face. It is in the individual's interest that the group to which he or she belongs remains intact and is not threatened. It is also in the individual's best interest that his or her standing and membership in the group is maintained. Thus there are constraints on the amount, kind and degree of self assertion on the part of the individual. The attempt to self assert and increase one's rank in the eyes of others is constrained by the necessity of keeping the group together, and of ensuring one's standing and belonging in it, both of which must be found within an interaction. As Scollon and Scollon point out:

> [w]e would like to emphasize that generally, as with speech acts in discourse, multiple strategies may be pursued in seeking to achieve the necessary interactional balance...[w]e assume...that any speech community or other communicative group will make use of multiple strategies that will vary from context to context (1981:183).

An example of this can be seen in TR06, a dinner time chat between Laura, Wendy and Ellen. Ellen is visiting Laura and Wendy at their apartment. They have just sat down to dinner and are discussing food. Laura asks Ellen what kippers are, and Ellen answers by describing kippers as similar to herring.

Ellen: Do you like pickled herring? You'd like kippers.
Laura: I love herring.
Ellen: If you loved pickled herring, you'd love 'em. I love pickled herring.
Wendy: I love herring. Do you like herring, Ellen?

Ellen: I love it.

This interchange becomes a survey of one another's food tastes. Laura and Wendy are long time friends, while Ellen is a relatively new acquaintance. Notice below how Ellen uses strategies of deference and solidarity to establish her social relationship in the group. She presents her own self-image as a member, one who has the same preferences, and simultaneously works to support the self-images that Laura and Wendy are presenting.

Ellen: *I love herring. I love chocolate.*
Laura: Wendy and I only live together because we love herring.
Ellen: *That's a better reason than many other reasons people live together, I think.*

Laura: That's really true. Because if one person likes herring and the other person doesn't, it can cause problems.
Ellen: *Yeah, it won't work.*

This interaction is characterized by the degree to which members sustain individuality or collectivity, deference or solidarity. Whether we observe systems operating between deference and solidarity, or individuals navigating between individual identity and status and group solidarity and belonging, we are observing the same phenomenon: the constant tension in human relationships of being a member of a group and simultaneously being an independent agent.

## 2.1. Face and repair

Speakers use politeness in language, according to Brown and Levinson, in their attempts to repair, redress or avoid situations in which an individual's face is potentially threatened. A face threatening act (FTA) results from one individual wanting something that would impinge upon another, such as a favor, reminder, suggestion or piece of advice. It could also be an act, which by its "nature runs contrary to the face wants of the addressee and/or the speaker." For example, a criticism, insult, or in some cases the honest truth would run contrary to the addressee's wants. As Brown and Levinson state, "any rational being would seek to avoid these face threatening acts, or will employ certain strategies to minimize the threat." These strategies of redressive action and repair often come hand in glove with the potential face threat. We see repair in conversation, for instance, in the way speakers "soften the blow" or hedge their opinions.

In the excerpt of TR01 below, Martin challenges the choice of agenda items set by the previous speaker, Laura, at a faculty meeting. We can see how he attempts to "soften the blow" of his interruption. Next to the founder and president, Martin is the highest ranking member of the institute. In the questionnaire, his name was given 85% of the time as someone others looked to as an advisor, leader, therapist, teacher or supervisor. Compare this to Laura, who was named by others only 59%. Martin is a grandparent, involved for 15 years, while Laura is a more recent arrival, a diplomate, which means that she graduated the program, had not been "grandparented" into it. Furthermore, Martin is 42 years old; Laura is 30. Martin thus clearly out-ranks Laura on every scale, however, Laura is the designated leader of the meeting, and has prepared an agenda that she is trying to present. She is also one of the administrators for the conference being discussed, and has limited authority to make decisions concerning the course and the faculty members involvement in it. Laura was ranked third by other members of the institute, behind the founder and Martin. She is the only non-grandparent to be listed in the top five positions, the only female, and clearly the youngest member of the top five. In spite of her lower rank relative to Martin, she has a high degree of local rank within the organization, though a lower institutional rank, as a woman, as a non-grandparent, in terms of her length of involvement, and due to her age.

Martin: I c- I can- I can tell you- I ca- can I say something?
Laura: Yeah.
Martin: I th- I think my need is uh (0.9) would be (1.2) to hear (0.7) what the
    people plan to    do, (.) more than like discuss (1.0) how you- I think that's up
Laura:              mhmm
Martin: to you guys, *how you* plan that. (0.5) *(0.5)*
Laura:              mhmm              mhmm
Martin: And I think that shouldn't be a democratic decision.
Laura: It's not. (0.6) I'm just announcing *it, so* that we could go on to the next
Martin:                                    ah so
Laura: thing, *(0.8)* which is (0.6) your ideas about curriculum. (0.6) I ju- just
Martin:      aha OK
Laura: wanted to bring that up because I- it's built *differently* then.
Martin:                                              alright.

Martin: Alright.

Martin's attempt to dispute Laura's choice of topic is a face threat which he tries to redress by going *off record*. As Brown and Levinson state,

> [a] communicative act is done off record if it is done in such a way that it is not possible to attribute only one clear communicative intention to the act. In other words, the actor leaves himself an "out" by providing himself with a number of defensible interpretations; he cannot be held to have committed himself to just one particular interpretation of his act (1978:216).

Martin's face-threat is off record in that he indirectly disputes her topic choice. Let us have a look in greater detail at Martin's strategies for challenging Laura's topic.

## 2.2. Lexical and syntactic choices

To begin with, Martin's explicit request to speak ("Can I say something?") is contextually marked behavior. Though Laura opened the meeting, it was not a formally mediated speech event. Thus, for Martin to specifically ask to speak is a negative politeness strategy; he acknowledges Laura as leader and attempts not to infringe upon her rights as speaker. Martin begins with the hedges "I think," and "My need would be." Hedges are usually indications of insecurity, as Lakoff (1975) has shown for women's speech. Certain discourse markers (cf. Schiffrin, 1987) including such words or phrases as "well," "I guess," "I mean," "y'know," may function similarly to hedges in that they soften, minimize or make vague the potential strength, force or accuracy of a speaker's statement. As Lakoff states:

> These hedges do have their uses when one really has legitimate need for protection, or for deference (if we are afraid that by making a certain statement we are overstepping our rights), ...(1975:54).

Martin's hedges are not due to the uncertainty of his statement, but to the fact that he is aware of the threat he poses to Laura's negative face by challenging her choice of topic.

Another method he uses to redress the FTA is to present his opinion in the first person, going off record by ensuring a degree of *subjectivity*. He states his opinion, not a fact. It is, as Brown and Yule (1983:89-90) state, "as if speakers feel obliged to offer some personal warrant for the statements they will make about the world." While it might be the speaker's personal opinion that what is said really is or should be considered a fact, saying so directly would result in reprisals. The opinion is therefore embedded in a personal reference such as "I think", "my idea", etc.

Stating an opinion is a speech act that might be a face threat in a given situation. In fact, any speech act which is a potential FTA such as a request, complaint, or criticism can be uttered as a subjective, personalized statement, momentarily weakening the force of the illocution, and hence the speech act. Thus, Martin says, "I think my need is to hear what the people have to say," instead of "I want to hear the people's ideas" or "Let's hear what the others have to say," both of which would be more directly confrontational to Laura's topic, and hence, to Laura. By phrasing his challenge as a wish ("My need is...to hear what the people have to say") he deletes a personal agent. Wanting, desiring, wishing, requesting something are intrinsic FTAs because they are an imposition upon the hearer. By deleting the agent and switching to the subjunctive modal "would," Martin goes off record by not directly claiming his wish.

Martin's specific set of hedges attempts to personalize his request, transforming his disagreement into a personal desire. It seems as if Martin switches strategies; he begins with a statement that appears on record ("My need is..."), but finishes off record with an insinuation that Laura and the others need not adhere to democratic policy. This is off record because it is not clear whether he disagrees because of his "need" for a different topic, or because he thinks it is best for Laura not to adhere to democratic tactics. One can only infer what he actually intends to say, for all "off record utterances are essentially indirect uses of language."

Martin uses deference strategies to preserve Laura's negative face-wants; he minimizes the imposition of his wishes by suggesting that they are Laura's wishes. Martin pays deference to Laura by exalting her scope of decision-making authority, she can make decisions without consulting the others. Deference strategies can be of two kinds; the speaker can humble himself or can exalt the other. Martin challenges the existing choice of topic and proposes a new one by other-exaltation: "I think that's up to you guys how you plan that, and I think that shouldn't be a democratic decision." In other words, he challenges the form of the meeting and thus the power of the temporary leader of the meeting by stating that the current leader(s) need not consult with others nor adhere to democratic principles. He exalts Laura in her role as decision maker by expanding her authority while questioning the decision to conduct the meeting in the way that she has chosen: "that's up to you....it shouldn't be a democratic decision." Yet the FTA that Martin commits, regardless of the strategies for repair, is to challenge Laura's topic. Paradoxically, by telling Laura that she has the power to make autocratic decisions, he is giving her the power to be powerful. He "permits" her to be more powerful, a paradoxical injunction that highlights his own authority and status.

Deference strategies, both other-exaltation and self-abasement, are used quite frequently in this meeting and found throughout the data. Deference politeness is common in cultures where it is used reciprocally between speakers and hearers separated by social distance and relative power, what Brown and Levinson (1978) refer to as high D (Distance) and P (Power) values. The social distance and relative power between members of this community are not substantial enough to consider it a deference culture. Its use in this instance, therefore, is strategic: it is used to hide the true intent of the speaker's wishes.

## 2.3. Pauses and self correction

Pauses in naturally occurring speech are of two kinds: grammatical and hesitation phenomena (Maclay and Osgood, 1959; Butterworth, Hine and Brady, 1977; Chafe, 1979).

A grammatical pause is one which may serve to identify linguistically relevant units, such as junctures located at the boundaries of phonemes, morphemes, words, phrases, and sentences (Maclay and Osgood, 1959:20) .

Grammatical pauses are differentiated from pauses which function as hesitation phenomena, together with filled pauses such as "um," "er," "mm" and the like, false starts and unfinished sentences. These phenomena are random non-linguistic items which have also been referred to as "planning pauses" or "lexical search pauses." While grammatical pauses serve a linguistic function, hesitation pauses "anticipate sudden increases in information or uncertainty in the message being produced" (Goldman-Eisler, 1958:67). The uncertainty in a message being produced can be due to many non-linguistic factors, including features of the situation. Brown and Levinson include prosodic and kinesic hedges in their classification of polite usage.

> Perhaps most of the verbal hedges can be replaced by (or emphasized by) prosodic or kinesic means of indicating tentativeness or emphasis. The raised eyebrow, the earnest frown, the umms and ahhs and hesitations that indicate the speaker's attitude towards what he is saying, are often the most salient clue to the presence of an FTA...(1978:177).

In the following segment from Martin's topic, there are a number of unusually long hesitation pauses. Note the difference in length between the grammatical pauses and the hesitation pauses, both filled and unfilled pauses. The hesitation pauses occur in the middle of a grammatical unit, in mid-idea. He is searching for the "right way to put it," and they indicate that what he is saying needs to be put delicately.

> Martin: I think my need is uh (0.9)- would be (1.2) to hear what the people plan
>    to *do, more* than like discuss (1.0) how you- I think that's up to you guys,
> Laura:  *mhmm*
> Martin: *how* you plan that. (0.5) *(0.5)*
> Laura:  *mhmm*                        *mhmm*

He has a filled pause of 0.9 seconds, followed by a self correction, then a pause of 1.2 seconds. This is an extremely long pause for a speaker within a turn. Later, he pauses again for 1.0 second and self corrects for a second time before concluding with, "I think that's up to you guys how you plan that." As Martin has a higher institutional rank than Laura, his hesitation phenomena display an uncertainty which is relative to the weight of his imposition.

## 2.4. Defending one's topic

Another means to measure the severity of Martin's face threat is by gauging Laura's reaction to it. How does she treat his attempt to change her topic? Despite Martin's redressive strategies, Laura's reactions indicate that a face threat has been made. Her response ("It's not") justifies her choice of topic, and indicates that Martin challenged more than her topic, but her role as leader, as well. In other words, the strategy Martin used to minimize his threat, i.e., telling her she need not adhere to democratic principles, increased its severity, for it implied that her leadership capacities were insufficient, that she had made a wrong assumption about the needs of the group. Laura, then, is doubly threatened: her topic and her leadership capacities are being questioned. Once Laura's status and topic have been challenged, she is left with two possibilities: she can either relinquish or defend them.

Martin: And I think that shouldn't be a democratic decision.
Laura: It's not. (0.6) I'm just announcing *it, so* that we could go on to the next
Martin:                                                        *ah so*
Laura: thing, *(0.8)* which is (0.6) your ideas about curriculum. (0.6) I ju- just
Martin:      *aha OK*
Laura: wanted to bring that up because I- it's built *differently* then.
Martin:                                                        *alright.*
Martin: Alright.

She counters his challenge by saying "it's not" (a democratic decision). She first denies, then minimizes and justifies her choice of topic. She minimizes through the use of a hedge, "just," de-emphasizing the significance of her topic. Similar to Martin's strategy, it is a deference defense. Whereas Martin used an other-exaltation deference ("it's up to you guys"), Laura uses self-abasement ("I'm *just* announcing it"). Self-abasement is a strategy whereby the speaker minimizes his or her own topic in order to avoid having it minimized by another's attacks. It is a form of self-defense to minimize the value of one's possessions, whether material or not, to divert others' attention, criticism or attack.

The particle "just" is, in varieties of English, a formulaic minimization of an utterance. In this example, Laura minimizes the importance of her topic as a way of defending it. *Just, only,* and *merely* minimize and de-emphasize what follows. As Brown and Levinson (1978:181) state, "one way of defusing the FTA is to indicate that Rx, the intrinsic seriousness of the imposition, is not in itself great...." Laura's next utterance is again a deference strategy. She defers to Martin by exalting his idea. In fact, she employs a device here reminiscent of the one that Martin used to redress his face threat to her. She explains her choice of topic by insisting that it is *his*. She does not insist on her topic; she relinquishes her claim to her topic, maintaining that it was his idea, and presenting her grounds for having introduced it, thus avoiding a direct collision with Martin. In fact, she combines minimizing and deference into one utterance:

It's not. I'm just announcing it, (minimizing)
so that we could go on to the next thing,

which is your ideas about curriculum. (deference)
I ju- just wanted to bring that up (minimizing)

The forms of deference Martin and Laura use, particularly other-exaltation and self-abasement, de-escalate the polarization between them. They use deference strategies to mutually minimize the weight of the impositions intrinsic in their face threats. He asserts that she need not consult others in her decision, and she asserts the intelligence and usefulness of her choice, and at the same time implies that her choice of topic was his choice of topic, too. In other words, she only wants what Martin wants. This is actually a blend of deference and solidarity politeness. She exalts his idea (deference) and claims that her wants are his wants (solidarity).

## 3. Politic verbal behavior

Explaining the foregoing interaction in terms *face threat* and *repair* implies an act-by-act sequence; something is done, damaged or broken which needs to be repaired (cf. Watts, 1989). Yet, as we have seen, repair and redress are evasive actions. Speakers use politeness strategies to avoid certain face threats, not only to repair something already done. In other words, the term *repair* is usually used for something already done, yet as evasive action it is generally used to avoid something *coming*. Thus, considering FTA and repair elements of relational work suggests that 1) they are part of an ongoing process, 2) utterances contain both threat and repair; they cannot be isolated or said to be in a causal relationship, and 3) the preservation of the group is as much a motivation for successful discourse as is presentation of self-image.

Brown and Levinson recognize this difficulty and suggest that FTAs be seen as *intentions* as well as *acts*. This is especially important when considering larger stretches of text, entire conversations, or any interchange above the level of a dyadic exchange. It is sometimes difficult to isolate the FTA within an interchange. Yet the term "face threatening act" leads us to believe the opposite. As Brown and Levinson themselves state,

> FTAs do not necessarily inhere in single acts (and hence the concept might be better labelled "face-threatening intention")....a higher level intention to issue a

criticism may be conveyed by a series of acts (and responses) that are not themselves FTAs (1978:238).

Despite reservations, the politeness model is an excellent tool for seeing how social relationships are signaled in language, and certainly the model cannot be faulted on the basis of terms alone. Yet it is important to discuss the terminology, for the connotation behind the terms evokes a sense of conversation as acts in a sequence. Empirical evidence shows that conversation is a continual and delicate balance of proximity and distance. Interactants,

> in any situation where the possibility of change in their social relationships exists, are constantly assessing the current "score"...and may make minute adjustments at any point in order to re-establish a satisfactory balance or to move the interaction in the desired direction towards greater closeness or distance (Brown and Levinson, 1978:236).

Polite language usage, whether it maintains positive or negative face, may not necessarily be in response to an overt act, but to an intention, a mood, or shared knowledge of past interaction.

Violations in conversational organization, such as interruptions, openings and closings are also FTAs, even though it is difficult to identify these structures as acts. For example, raising a topic implicitly challenges the preceding topic as well as the participants engaged in that topic. To say, however, that raising a topic is an FTA, while possibly true, misses the point; the larger idea is that the entire interchange balances the delicate web of interpersonal relationships, of the individual's position and his or her relationship to others. Therefore, in applying Brown and Levinson's model to our data, it might be useful to keep in mind that speakers may or may not commit FTAs; there may be challenging or threatening intentions or knowledge that call for positive or negative politeness in language usage. What the data reveal is not necessarily FTAs (though it may be the case) but *politic* verbal behavior, that is, verbal strategies that attempt to maintain a state of equilibrium and stability in the interchange (and hence relationship) by maintaining proximity or distance.

## 3.1. Going off-record

Another example of the careful balance between proximity and distance is evident in the following interchange between Ulrike and Laura, excerpted from TR01. Laura, an organizer for an upcoming course, is explaining to other faculty members how the course will be organized. She is the momentary resource person. Ulrike, another faculty member, asks her a question concerning the days of the course which have been designated "seminar days." Only four out of thirteen faculty members were asked to lead these special sessions. As an organizer, Laura knows that Ulrike was not asked to lead any of these days and perceives this information as possibly threatening to Ulrike. Furthermore, Ulrike has asked this question in front of an entire group, many of whom were also not chosen. In terms of institutional rank, Ulrike surpasses Laura: she is 44 years old; she is one of the original "grandparents," and she has been involved twice as long as Laura. However, in terms of local rank, Laura was given a higher ranking from her peers than Ulrike, having been named 59% to Ulrike's 20%. As we look at the text, has Ulrike threatened Laura's face? Laura feels put on the spot, and defers, indirectly. Notice how she answers Ulrike's question obliquely.

Ulrike: Also b- can you explain a little bit about those seminar days?
    0.6
Laura: The first seminar day is gonna be led by Peter, (0.5) *(.)*
[Ulrike:                                               *yuh*]
    and uh (0.8) the actual stru::cture of the seminar days is up to (0.8) the seminar
    (0.6) leader.(.) *(0.7)* They (.) do what they want. The second two da::ys (0.8)--
Ulrike:            *aha*
Kim: The last day Peter's doing    *also.*
Laura:                         *And* th- the last day Peter's doing too.
Ulrike: mh *mm*
Alain:      *I thou*ght it was George and me?
Laura: Yeah.
George: We're doing it on Thursday.=
Laura: = B*ut it w-was*
Alain:      *{ah} on Thurs*day. And  th *en Pe*ter does it on the
George:                         *Yeah.*
Alain:    last day.
George: Yeah.
Laura:    Yeah.

Laura, though the resource person, does not satisfy Ulrike's request for an explanation about the seminar days. Rather than continue logically by stating who is going to lead the second, third and fourth days, she shifts topics slightly. Later on in the text, Laura explicitly asks Kim, another organizer, for help. By taking herself out of the role of resource person, she escapes possible reprisals for the potentially threatening information. Thus, her rhetorical strategy is to be vague and insufficiently informative in order to avoid responsibility. She violates Grice's (1975) maxim of relevance, failing to provide the expected information about the leaders of the second, third and fourth days. Instead, she discusses their structure. Her frequent pauses, especially those within a tone unit, indicate that she is hedging; she does not want to take responsibility for the truth of her utterance.

Laura: The first seminar day is gonna be led by Peter, *(0.5)* (.)
[Ulrike:                                                        *yuh*]
and uh (0.8) the actual stru::cture of the seminar days is up to (0.8) the seminar
(0.6) leader.

We might interpret her hesitancy, as indicated by the frequent pauses, as a sign of not wanting to commit herself to a position. As she is therefore not fulfilling the role of resource person, Kim, a fellow organizer, comes in at the point where she hesitates:

Laura: (.) do what they want. The second two da::ys (0.8)--
Kim: The last day Peter's doing also.

Kim volunteers the information that Laura neglected, and takes over the role that Laura is avoiding. The fact that Alain comes in right after Kim clarifies that Peter is doing the last day as well, confirms that being accountable and providing information in a situation where it might be threatening to do so brings reprisals. As soon as an organizer committed herself, someone came in and made her accountable for the information.

Violating the maxims of relevance and of quantity, as Laura has done, produces confusion. Alain and Ulrike request clarification. Alain thought he was doing the fourth day when in fact he and George had been asked to lead the third day. But when Alain questions this, Laura once again hedges, violating the maxim of relevance, and gives the inappropriate answer, "Yeah." This time George comes in and provides the information that Laura is expected to provide. Rather than clearing up the situation, it seems that this question and answer series is muddying the waters. Instead of getting the information she requests from one speaker, Ulrike is getting bits and pieces of the information from different speakers. Going back to the interchange, Laura's abdication of the role of resource person leaves the situation confused:

Ulrike: Also was-- uh (0.7) thursday isch de zweit *letschte?*
Laura:                                       *Yeah.*
Ulrike: George und Alain.
Laura: George und Alain.
    0.9
Laura: And the second day is uh (0.8) [low to Kim] Yvonne and Martin. (0.6) Is that right?
Kim: Mmhm.
Laura: Yeah.
    1.0
Laura: And the structure's left up to them, (1.0) in terms of what they actually want to do. But the needs from the participants' point of view, (0.7) *i:s* (.) to: ha::ve
[Ulrike:                                             *ja*]
Laura: experiential (0.5) demonstrations of process work. A lot of them have never seen it,(.) *or* they've been to only seminars and they'd like to see it do *ne,*
*(.)* in
[Ulrike:       *ja*                                    *mhm*]
front of the gro*up.* They'd like personal experience (0.7) And then on the last
[Ulrike:      *mhm*]
two days, *(.) that* same focus but with an integrative(.) feel to it, that it- that
[Martin:     *mhm*]
Laura: they have a sense of like how to integrate it and take it back.

Ulrike attempts to get clarity and reformulates the information in Swiss German: "Also, was, was, Thursday isch de zweit letschte?" (Then, what...what -- Thursday is the second to last [day]?) Her utterance is an explicit request, which puts Laura in the position of having to provide the information that the second day is to be led by Yvonne and Martin. Once again, she relinquishes her duty to be accountable and defers to Kim, asking her *sotto voce* if the information is correct. Thus, by default, she assigns the role of resource person (and its accountability) to Kim. Later in the meeting, Ulrike, once again, requests information about teachers' roles during the seminar days:

Ulrike: And uh (.) we other teachers, (.) can we just go there or do we have to speak with the:: semi:na::r lea::ders? O::r --
    1.0
Ulrike: How do you want to have that?

Sylvia: I think actually it's- would be (.) *begruesst\* (0.9) if as many (0.8) people
*as pos*sible *would* come.
Karen: *sure*
George: *sure*
Kim: Come.
Laura: Come.

Ulrike states her question hesitantly, as indicated by frequent pauses
and drawn out words: "and uh (.) we we other teachers, uh (.) can we
just go there or do we have to speak with the:: semi:na::r lea::ders? O:r
--". The long intraturn pauses, self correction, and the lengthening of
"seminar leaders" show that Ulrike is insecure about her question. The
fact that no one comes in to provide her with the information at the end
of her question indicates that there is indeed good reason for her
insecurity. A whole second goes by without a response. This is unusual
for two reasons. First, throughout the entire meeting, interturn pauses
were infrequent, and usually brief, averaging a half second or so. Second,
questions usually get answered promptly. After a full second pause,
Ulrike sees that she is not getting a response, and prompts an answer:
"how do you want to have that?" Finally, Sylvia comes in with a type of
response:

I think actually it's - it would be (.) begruesst - (0.9) if as many (0.8) people as
possible would come.

The speaker's insecurity is demonstrated in the use of long intraturn
pauses, what are called *lexical search pauses*. These pauses indicate that
Sylvia is searching for the "right" word. Lexical search pauses can be
differentiated from the more typical pauses occurring at tone unit
boundaries, indicating a finished thought, idea or syntactic unit in that
they occur in mid-idea or in the middle of a syntactic unit. An indication
that Sylvia, too, not just Laura, attempts to go off record in providing
Ulrike with the requested information is in her case of code switching.
She uses the German *begruesst* (*greeted; welcomed*) rather than the
English equivalent. This interchange shows a situation which can clearly
be considered threatening in Brown and Levinson's sense of the term,
even though there is no specific face threatening act to speak of. The
speakers in the above example use evasive language: hesitation, hedges,
reiterations, deferments, indirection, code switches and pauses, pointing
to a delicate, potentially embarrassing or politically difficult issue. Laura

is indirect and tries to avoid going on record by providing neither sufficient nor relevant information for Ulrike's request.

Interactions in which interlocutors use evasive and politic language indicate a situation which is threatening due to some background information, the constellation of participants, or a future intention, not only a particular act or request that needs redressive action. In the last example, trying to isolate a particular face threat as a reason for Laura's politic behavior would unnecessarily limit our analysis and interpretation of the situation. The verbal behavior in this interaction indicates a possible face threatening act at many levels. Simply divulging the information that certain teachers were not chosen for this task is a potential FTA. Moreover, the administrators responsible for communicating the information about who leads the seminars days are of lower rank than the trainers. And finally, the reasons why certain teachers are chosen over others are not publicly given. This is the delicate situation in the background. Laura is afraid to take responsibility for her utterance because of reprisals from Ulrike and other higher ranking teachers who were not asked to lead the seminar days.

## 4. Speech situations and severity of FTAs

Both excerpts above are from a speech situation marked by a high degree of formality. In smaller and less formal situations such as a party, chat or small group, where there is minimal social distance, such as between close friends, speakers are freer to impose on each others' wants. In large meetings where an agenda or task needs to be addressed, and where there is greater social distance between at least some of the participants, there is a greater constraint on the interactions, and participants are more concerned with lessening the severity of FTAs and with using politic verbal behavior. Other constraints of situation and setting which speakers can manipulate include the necessities of the agenda, time pressure, number of people present, etc. For instance, speakers may deliberately use features of the situation to pressure the other participants, as did the chair of the meeting in TR04 below:

- Let's talk about it in public.
- Let's do it for 10 minutes and then it's over.

In order to weigh the severity of face threats and to analyze how speakers negotiate them, features of the speech situation must be considered. There is more to the severity of a face threat than relative power, social distance and weight of the imposition. Actors in one situation will act differently towards each other in another situation. What might be face threatening behavior between two speakers in public, might not be in private between the same two speakers. Goffman (1959) discusses this phenomenon as performance and impression management. Let us now look at how speakers navigate self-assertion and the need to minimize FTAs across a variety of different speech situations.

## 4.1. Network variables and interaction

An interaction is situated in a particular context and carried out between participants in specific relationships to each other. The meanings in an interaction must therefore be interpreted against the backdrop of the local social features and norms of the speakers. In close-knit networks, messages cannot be understood only on a semantic level; contextualization cues which signal how the message is to be interpreted, as well as the social features of the interactants, their relationships and the momentary situation all contribute to an understanding of the utterance. Because many of the social features of a group are based on norms and values specific to the particular group, the social features of the society at large, such as socio-economic class, do not always help us understand the verbal interactions between members. Thus, network analysis situates the verbal and nonverbal interactions between interactants by depicting the relationships and the patterns of interaction and cooperation between them.

When communication between a group of people occurs over a long period of time, with a degree of regularity, communicative conventions arise, marking specific activities, ways of speaking, and norms that serve to distinguish those in the network from those outside it. Furthermore, the shared norms, values, backgrounds and activities are reflected in and perpetrated by forms of speaking, and also through interactional styles and strategies, themes of talk and style of argumentation. Members' knowledge of the group's linguistic tokens and conventions is reflected in the way they exploit them to signal affiliation with the group or to dissociate themselves from it.

Furthermore, members' effectiveness within the group depends on their control over a range of communicative options and on their knowledge of the signalling potential that these options have in alluding to shared history, values and mutual obligations (Gumperz, 1982:206).

Interactions can be characterized according to whether or not they occur between members of the same network cluster or subgroup. Intimacy, or minimal social distance, is directly related to the degree of polite language usage. Rank, status and negotiation for power underlie the interactions between people. These variables, however, are only meaningful

to the extent that the actors think it is mutual knowledge between them that these variables have some particular values. Thus these are not intended as sociologists' ratings of actual power, distance, etc., but only as actors' assumptions of such ratings, assumed to be mutually assumed, at least within certain limits (Brown and Levinson, 1978:80-1).

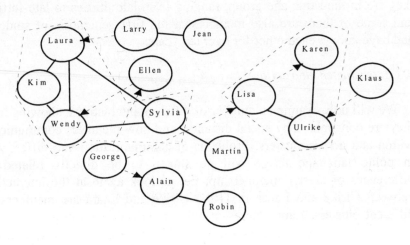

*Figure 3.1. Sociogram and clusters*

As discussed earlier, a cluster is a portion of the larger network which exhibits a density greater than that of the rest of the network. Network density was defined earlier in this study as the number of reciprocal namings, and the number of namings of institute members as opposed to non-members. In this community, social acquaintances are overwhelmingly linked through organizational, academic and professional activities. Thus the links between the members of a cluster are reciprocal (each member names those who name that member as well) and multiplex (links which describe many different types of connections: friendship, work colleagues, neighbors, etc.). The network sociogram of the community used in the data reveal two clusters.

There is one particularly strong cluster, of which the members are five women. All the ties in this cluster are reciprocal and multiplex. They are all in the same age group, late twenties and early thirties, and are peers at the institute. In addition, four of the women sit on an administrative committee together, and four of them attended university together in the United States and have known each other for over 10 years. There is another, less dense cluster which is also comprised of women.[12] There are fewer reciprocal social namings in this cluster than in the one above, but the women also have multiplex relationship ties to each other. They see each other socially; they meet regularly for peer supervision and training; they are in the same age group, ranging from late thirties to late-forties; and some of them are also members of the first generation of students and have known each other for over ten years.

## 4.2. Intercluster interaction

We will now examine a number of different interactions, showing how they are constrained by social distance, and how members communicate within and across clusters. Problems of communication and differences in polite language usage will be shown to be directly related to differences of cluster membership. Let us look again at the interaction between Ulrike and Laura in TR01. Ulrike and Laura are members of different clusters. Laura represents the organizational sub-group which called the meeting. Ulrike is a trainer, older than Laura, and one of the first generation of students. Thus, she has a higher institutional status

---

[12] The fact that the only clusters are comprised of women is not, I believe, accidental. It would be worth investigating this more closely. L. Milroy (1980) also found significant differences in sex in his study of verbal interaction within working class and lower class neighborhoods.

than Laura. Laura's position as organizer and momentary resource person, however, puts her temporarily in a position of power.

Ulrike: Also b- can you explain a little bit about those seminar days?

0.6

Laura: The first seminar day is gonna be led by Peter.

0.5

Ulrike: Yuh

Laura: And uh (0.8) the actual stru::cture of the seminar days is up to (0.8) the
seminar (0.6) leader. (.) *(0.7)* They (.) do what they want. The second two

[Ulrike:                                  *aha*]

Laura: da::ys--

Notice that Ulrike formulates the question with a hedge, the diminutive, "a little bit," which minimizes the weight of the imposition. Hence, her question must be an imposition. The force of an imposition is proportionate to the degree of social distance between participants, therefore, the question indicates a lack of intimacy between Ulrike and Laura. Further, as we know, Laura hedges and does not give a complete answer.

The social distance in this interaction is apparent when compared to other requests between members at the same meeting. Later on in the meeting, after an hour of heated discussion about curriculum, the members are close to an agreement to begin the course with methods, rather than theory. George suddenly objects and states that he had wanted to start his class with something theoretical. Notice Martin's response:

George: Well (0.7) we- we thought like for the first se- the first session of process
theory, (0.6) uh (0.5) like to do things like metaphoric- like metaphors for
process, (0.8) and like uh (0.8) just give 'em a really strong idea about what
process is, (2.0) a::nd uh (0.8) the first week not to get too technical
about *uh (2.1)- but really to- to-*

Martin:    *uhu how-- about uh (0.9)-*

George: Yeah?

Martin: How bout changing that? (0.6) And- and doing channels and edges in the
first week?

The interaction between George and Martin can be explained in several ways. In a sense, Martin face-threatens George by directly requesting that he change his plans. Though George and Martin do not belong to the same cluster, they do have similar status in the organization. They are both first generation members and have had more social contacts with each other than Ulrike and Laura have had. Thus, the power and distance variables are more minimal than those between Ulrike and Laura. This on record face threat might also be a suspension of polite language usage due to the need to exchange information and arrive at decisions in a relatively short time span. As Scollon and Scollon explain, meetings are situations

> in which a high amount of information needs to be exchanged over a relatively brief period. Because each act of information exchange would tend to produce R[ank of imposition]s of some value and many of these are expected, P[ower] and D[istance] would have to be kept at an absolute minimum. To insure the easy flow of information with minimum risk to face, a system of solidarity politeness would be needed (1981:178).

Conferences, meetings and military operations function on this principle. In the meeting, George's objection comes towards the end; the meeting has lasted over an hour and the participants wanted to come to a closure. Rather than get sidetracked on an objection, we might guess that Martin opts for going on record in order to expedite the decision.

Returning to Ulrike and Laura, Ulrike asks Laura whether or not other teachers may sit in on the seminar days led by other teachers.

Ulrike: And uh (.) we- we other teachers, uh (.) can we just go there or do we have
  to speak with the: semi:na::r lea::ders? O:r --
  1.0
Ulrike: How do you want to have that?
Sylvia: I think actually it's- it would be (.) *begruesst*, (0.9) if as
many (0.8) people *as*
Karen:              *Sure*
Sylvia: possible would come.
George: Sure.
Kim: Come.
Laura: Come.

Ulrike hedges with hesitation phenomena, filled pauses and drawn-out words. Her question is followed by a 1.0 second pause in which there is no response. Her prompt for an answer ("How do you want that?") is overlapped by Sylvia's answer. Sylvia's indirect answer, though, betrays her unwillingness to go on record: "it would be *begruesst* if as many people as possible would come." As Sylvia is an organizer, not a teacher leading a seminar day, she cannot state with certainty whether other teachers are welcomed or not. Similar to Laura, she is in the position of disseminating information which her status does not allow her to take responsibility for. Her statement reveals this in the absence of a direct agent; no one directly "welcomes" people. Here, we clearly see how the organizers' ability to be informative is constrained by situational and relational factors. Laura has to impart information to others of higher status, power and greater social distance about their rights and obligations. Going on record means taking responsibility for decisions which might incur the disapproval of others in a more powerful position. Hence, her only option is to insufficiently fulfil her role as resource person.

### 4.3. Intracluster interaction

Contrast the above situations to TR05 below, in which members of the same cluster, Laura, Wendy and Kim are discussing the cost of room and board for financial aid students coming to Zurich. Kim proposes that food might cost approximately 25 francs per person per day.

Kim: Yeah, (2.1) well let's be- then we'll be very loose, say twenty five a day,
    (1.2) twenty five ti::mes (1.1) -
Wendy: Seven--
Laura: TWENTY FIVE FRANCS FOR FOOD A DAY?
Kim: Yeah.
    2.1
Wendy: Twenty, twenty *five*.
Kim:              *Whad*da you think *about it? You think --*
Wendy:                      *Yeah. Whadda you* think? It's too
    much?
Laura: Let's hope they're all skinny.
    0.8
Wendy: You think that's not enough?
Laura: NO. (0.8) Breakfast, lunch and dinner.
    2.2

Capital letters indicate volume. Laura challenges Kim's proposal loudly and in a skeptical tone. The force of the face threat is carried not so much by the disagreement, but by its indirection; the prosody is on record as doubt and a challenge, but she fails to provide reasons for her doubt. She repeats Kim's proposal with a tone of disbelief, in a questioning manner, without officially going on record as disagreeing. Declining to state her own opinion leaves a moment of confusion. Kim and Wendy read her statement differently. Wendy reacts by imagining that Laura thinks it is too little ("You think that's not enough?"), while

Kim thinks just the opposite ("It's too much?"). Between participants of greater social distance and power differences, this would be a bald face threatening act. The closeness of the ties between these participants allows for direct confrontation. However, a closer look at the interaction reveals that Laura's question has resulted in a face threatening situation.

Directly after her question, there is a pause of 2.1 seconds. After this initial silence, the others begin to challenge and finally override Laura's objection:

Kim: Well, depends how ya (1.5) do it.
Wendy: You don't think twenty five- I mean now- *y-you-- (.)* think they're eating
     out
Laura:                                      *That's like a-*
Wendy: three meals a day. (2.8) For eating out three meals a day it's low,(1.5)
     but--
     1.6
Laura: Wh-where else are th *ey gonna stay?*
Wendy:                    *They're gonna* be living somewhere.

The tone of Laura's objections changes from the initial loudness of "Twenty five francs for food a day?" to the hesitant objection above: "Wh- where else are they gonna stay?" It appears that she begins to waver from her initial standpoint. Her tone is more uncertain, observable in the self-corrections. She tries to back up her disagreement with reasons but is actually finding that she might be in the wrong.

Laura: How dya- Maybe we- they won- maybe we'll have to- oh. (0.7) They will
     be living somewhere, right. (0.7)
Laura: But that me *ans-*
Wendy:        *They* could bring sandwiches with them.
Laura: Yeah, but that means that like- (2.0) we::ll (.)--
Kim: I *don't know, if you bring s- (0.8) I think a sandwich* for ??? is fine.
Laura: *you could like never- you could like never go out.*
Wendy I think twenty five francs--
Laura: They could like never go out or something.

Both Wendy and Kim form an alliance against Laura's position and go on record refuting Laura's initial objection:

Wendy: I think twenty five a day is-is OK.
Kim: I think so t *oo.*
Wendy:        *These* are poor people. They're used to like (2.1) eating
     sandwiches.
Kim: Umm we eat sandwiches too. I don't eat- who eats big lunches?
Kim: *I- I can* eat well on twenty five francs a day.

Wendy:  *I think--*
    0.9
Kim: I can eat really well.
Wendy: I think twenty five francs a day is OK.

In conclusion, the severity of an imposition or a face threatening act depends on the social distance and power between participants. The greater the social distance, the more polite the language usage. Thus, the occurrence of a face threat sometimes points to participants of close social distance. This is such a situation where the closeness between the members allows for the bald on record verbal behavior.

## *4.4. Interaction in formal settings*

Where the social distance and power between participants is great, dissent and disagreement are voiced indirectly. In large meetings participants whisper and use nonverbal means such as exchange of glances, eye contact, and gestures to express disagreement or conflict with the proceedings. As most of the recordings were audio recordings, the rich corpus of nonverbal interaction is necessarily excluded from this discussion. In TR01, however, a few participants began to whisper back and forth at one point during the discussion. Ulrike had just asked whether other teachers could attend the seminar days, and the floor divided into simultaneous conversations. Another teacher, Klaus, of similar status to Ulrike, asks whether or not teachers are obliged to attend the Friday afternoon group process class. Klaus, a native Swiss German speaker, gropes for the right term:

Klaus: Ju- just- but we- we are greeted but not- we- we are not obliged- but we are
    uh o- obliged to uh (0.6)--
Kim: Warmly invited.
Klaus: Invited. I see. Huh.
Kim: Warmly invi *ted.*
Klaus:          *Warm*ly invited. (0.6) uh (0.6) only the Friday afternoon is uh
    (0.9) meant that we (.) should be there?

Kim volunteers the expression "warmly invited." The situation is similar to that of Ulrike and Laura above. The organizers want to tell the teachers that they actually should go to the group process class. However, they lack the status to make it an "official" order. Thus, they use the expression *warmly invited*. The other teachers laugh at this blatant form of indirectness, and take it to mean that teachers are indeed expected to go. Meanwhile, two other teachers, both of whom are leading the seminar days, whisper to others sitting near by. They joke about the term *warmly invited*, and one of them whispers to another, "You're all *warmly invited* to stay out," whereupon a number of others sitting close by begin to laugh.

What do these observations reveal about politic interaction and social distance? Dissent or disagreement is not easy to raise in a large group. The careful speaking style of the organizers in the meeting, compared to their interactional style when they are alone, indicates that differences in speaking styles can be predicted, and communication difficulties understood by network structure, in particular social distance (clusters) and power. Polite language usage decreases in situations where participants have very little social distance.

All the group members equivocate, hesitate and choose off record strategies around certain issues. There appear to be taboo subjects which fall outside what can be discussed openly. The types of interactional styles and problems in the examples show how conflict or tension is rarely made explicit in a group. The participants voice their objections, feelings and disagreements in whispers, as jokes, and in carefully chosen terms ("warmly invited"), and also by going off-record, being vague and deferring to others. Careful, politic behavior is used in public to maintain the web of relationships and to smooth over impositions and face threats occurring between clusters and statuses.

## 5. Manipulating deference and solidarity strategies

As we have now seen, politic verbal behavior is a way to describe the careful negotiation of speakers' self-asserting, raising topics, challenging others' topics, etc., and maintaining the delicate web of interrelationships. It seems clear that politic behavior is more than sequential acts of FTAs and repairs; rather, it is a careful balancing act, a sophisticated set of strategies used to promote oneself, to respect the social distance and status between interactants, and to preserve the fabric of the relationships within the group.

Deference and solidarity are more than strategies speakers use to negotiate interaction; they are also used wittingly as strategies to achieve political power. We shall now investigate rhetorical devices speakers use to further their own standing and status in the group. In a further example from TR01, Alain, who has the same institutional status as Martin, introduces a new topic. The others had been discussing Martin's idea, and Alain's idea is slightly different. As he tables his topic, he is sitting just outside the circle where the rest of the faculty sits.

Alain: We could do something like that, like- uh (0.9) we could go a little bit further in the idea of Martin, (0.6) give certain themes (0.5) per week, (0.5) that should be treated around uh (1.3)- that uh (0.5)- classes should be arranged around those themes. (1.1) Something like that.
Laura: mhmm.
   1.3

There is an intrinsic FTA in introducing a new topic or shifting to another one in the midst of the discussion around Martin's idea. Alain minimizes the threat to Martin by presenting his new topic as "going a little bit further in the idea of Martin," i.e. exalting the other. His topic is Martin's topic. Alain "packages" the new topic, so to speak, as the old one. He suggests that it is an extension of, and hence the same as Martin's. Martin is thus put in a position where he must agree; otherwise he would be disagreeing with his own idea. Alain does not hedge in the same way Martin did. It appears that he launches directly into the topic, in contrast to Martin, who began with hesitation phenomena and hedges. If we take a close look at Alain's utterance, however, we see that he employs different hedges; he holds the floor without having given the main thrust of his idea. He begins with, "we could do something like that" and then follows with. "we could go a little bit further in the idea of Martin."

Not being a native speaker of English, Alain uses the demonstrative pronoun "that" to refer to the following idea. He manages to hold the floor because the main argument has not yet been delivered. Similar to beginning a sentence with a subordinate clause, Alain's strategy introduces the topic without revealing it: "Listen folks, what's coming is important." This is sometimes used as a turn-taking device when many parties bid for the floor. It enables the speaker to simultaneously claim the floor by speaking and to out-wait the others until he or she is sure of the others' attention. The speaker is talking and thus making a claim to speak, but withholds the main idea of the argument in order that it is not lost in the simultaneous talk.

## 5.1. Rhetorical strategies

Another example of how speakers manipulate deference and solidarity strategies concerns the interactional style of the highest ranking members of the institute. In contrast to the two relatively dense clusters of women we discussed previously, the four highest-ranking trainers of the institute are men who show only one reciprocal or multiplex tie with another community member; in each case the tie is to a partner or spouse. Though they occasionally name others or are named uni-directionally, they cannot be said to belong to a cluster within the network. They were the most frequently named by other members as therapists, teachers, consultants and community leaders. They are thus ranked first, second, fourth and fifth respectively in the organization. This is rather typical for the social pattern of a business or professional community; it is marked by hierarchical stratification between members in which high ranking members tend to have more social distance between themselves and lower status members. We must remember that the sociogram (figure 3.1) depicts social ties only. If we were to depict a sociogram showing the amount and reciprocity of business or information ties in the community, these higher-ranking members would be a part of a dense cluster as well. If these higher-ranking members are characterized by greater social distance to other members, then we might expect to find more polite language usage between them and other members. The data, however, show a particular interactional style in which these higher status members manipulate deference and solidarity politeness in order to achieve political effectiveness. In TR01 below, teachers are discussing a proposal to re-structure the curriculum. In the example below, Martin, the highest ranking member present, summarizes the discussion to date and illustrates the new proposal with a concrete example. Notice the amount and kinds of listener response he receives.

Martin: Ja, (.) for example (0.7) that you're still a- that you're still able (0.6) to like
   do your own course, the w *ay you* want to do it, (0.7) but it's more like a focus.
Robin:                                    *uhuh*
Laura: mhmm mhmm

Ulrike: mhmm mh *mm*
Klaus:                *mhmm*, yeah.
Martin: For example, *I'm thinking-* uh (1.0) *for me-* uh (3.1) it would be helpful,
   (0.9) is- if in the first week,(0.8) people get like an overall idea (0.7)about what
   it is that we're doing, (0.8) with some like basic concepts, (0.6) (1.3)
Laura:                          *mhm*
Ulrike:                          *mhm*
Martin: and uh (1.4) and-and maybe we should like- (1.2) I think that would help
   me the most- *me personally,* (0.8) (0.9) that uh (0.6) they have an idea
[Laura:          *mhm*]
   what the process work means, and about (0.7) primary and secondary processes,
   and edges, that would be enough,(0.5) (1.0) and uh (1.7) and tha-(0.9) that we
      *some*how can
[Ulrike:  *mhm*]
Martin: like coordinate, (0.7) how to *trichtern* that *ein*, (1.0) how to (1.7) pour it
   down their throats i *n the first week,* (1.2)
Ulrike:                  *[low laugh]*
Alain:                          *pouri ng--*
Laura:                          *mhm*
Lisa:                          *[giggle]*
Martin: that like not everybody is doing the whole thing again, or something like
   that.

The effectiveness of Martin's contribution can be measured by the
amount of listener response he receives. His joke, "how to trichtern that
ein" (how to "funnel," i.e. pour that in) is acknowledged by the others
through their laughter. Martin's strategic use of humor, personal markers
and story telling devices make his utterance rhetorically as well as
politically effective. He is able to bring the others to an agreement on the
topic. Martin's strategies include phrasing his idea as a personal wish:
   I'm thinking, for me, it would be helpful...
   I think that would help me the most, me personally.
   He outlines the idea in a personal manner, appealing to the others by
using pronouns such as you, we and us:
   You're still able to like do *your* own course, the way *you* want to do it.
   Maybe *we* should like...
   *We* somehow can like coordinate...
   These in-group markers claim common ground with others (Brown
and Levinson, 1978), i.e. speaking as one of the members: we, you, us.
This strategy is often used to redress or soften the weight of an FTA;
here, however, it is politic language which helps the speaker achieve

political effectiveness. This type of utterance, found in stratified societies, works on the principle whereby

> the reciprocal exchange of the T [tu] pronoun [is] associated with the lower groups, classes or castes in their ingroup interactions, and a tendency for the reciprocal use of V [Vous] to be associated with upper strata (Brown and Levinson, 1979:322).

The joke, "how to trichtern that ein," works due to different linguistic and non-linguistic facts. First, it is a switch of codes: he inserts the verb and particle *ein trichtern* (funnel into) into an English sentence structure. This is a co-occurrence violation. His ability to code-switch a particle verb of German into English syntax demonstrates "local team" membership (cf. Gumperz, 1972a, 1982). Understanding his joke required in-group membership, i.e. the ability to understand both English and German. Additionally, his joke functions as a solidarity marker with the other teachers by evoking an image which calls upon prior knowledge of the teaching profession. Understanding his joke requires in-group membership on two accounts: as a bilingual speaker of English and German, and as a fellow teacher. An in-joke like his is similar to jargon or slang which "may evoke all the shared associations and attitudes that he and [the others] both have toward that [subject]..."(Brown and Levinson, 1978:116). Finally, the concept of pouring something down students' throats is an ironic comment. Martin makes explicit a background judgement about teaching and learning that usually only those students or teachers critical of the education process make. By betraying a critical attitude towards teaching, he distances himself from the role of teacher and authority and shows himself to be a member of the "masses." His ability to manipulate the codes and norms of the community to signal in-group membership and simultaneously to invite other teachers into the in-group is characteristic of leaders and higher ranking members of a particular community. In his work on inner city youths, Labov (1972b) shows

> some special uses of language among Black youths in New York which involved exchanges of ritual insults as a competitive game for prestige. ...Outsiders or group marginals are unlikely to understand the rules, and the correct employment of the rules in a verbal contest is then an indication of membership in the Black community (Brown and Levinson, 1979:310).

Every community has its own local and specific ritual games or norms that can be exploited for social and interpersonal meanings. In this case, Martin's joke brought about an enthusiastic response from the others and provided an image for the new idea the others were striving to establish. George, another higher ranking member, makes a contribution later in the meeting that receives support and encouragement from the others.

George: I wanna- I wanna s- say something based on- like for me this was like a really good experience, this uh (.) German intensive, with a theme,(0.5) *(0.5)*

Karen:                                                                                          *mhm*

George: because uh (0.5) usually when I do theory, I just (0.5) do theory, and like having to do it(.) from the standpoint of symptoms, was li- I had to restructure the whole thing, (1.0) and teach it in a completely different way. (0.7) So it seems like if you're uh (0.6)- if you have uh (1.6)- you have movement work, you have dreamwork, uh (2.0) video analysis, group process things, there's a chance (0.8) to talk about the specific (0.6) *uh (1.4)* way that edges,

Alain:                                                                                      *exactly*

George: for instance, if you're talking about edges in the second- in the second week, (0.6) you can really be very specific about how edges work in

         tho*se areas--*

Karen:    *so the move*ment class will talk about movement edges,

Similar to Martin, George begins his suggestion with a story of his own experiences: "like for me this [past course] was a really good experience." His method of explaining his idea is also similar to Martin's; he addresses the others personally and formulates ideas as personal wishes and experiences:

For me this was like a really good experience...

Usually when I do theory...

I had to restructure the whole thing, and teach it in a completely different way.

If you're going to be talking about edges in the second week...

Both George and Martin use the construction "for me" to express their views:

Martin: I'm thinking, for me, it would be helpful...

George: For me this was like a really good experience...

George's idea receives support from the others. Alain, another high status community member supports his contribution ("exactly") and another teacher, Karen, overlaps his utterance by supporting and clarifying his idea, helping to develop the topic further. Later on in the same meeting, Martin again makes a strong case for re-structuring the curriculum, using concrete examples, and addressing the others directly:

Martin: so what you think? That- like you said that- like the majority of the people
   (0.6) will come, and they (0.6) probably will have very- they're like  beginners.(.)
              *(1.1)* They're gonna be in a shock about (.) being in *Switz*erland,
Wendy:    *mhm*
Kim       *mhm*
Laura:                                                                              *yeah*
Martin: (1.0) getting to know all kinds of new people that they hadn't known
   before. (0.6) *(.) It's* gonna be a big thing. So I think that the first week (0.6) we
   should
[Laura:          *mhm*]
   Martin: take it like a little bit easy, (.)   *(.) with* the content.
George:                              *mhm*
Laura:                                *mhm*

Notice how he asks the others what they think about his idea: "So what
(do) you think?" and then attributes the motivation for his idea to
someone else: "Like *you* said that like the majority of the people". Here
Martin goes beyond simply claiming common ground. He actually
presents his idea *as if it were someone else's*. In the other curriculum
meeting, TR04, Peter, the highest ranking member present, tries to get
the other teachers to focus on self-criticism. He uses the same strategies
of bringing in personal experiences and using personalized subjects and
in-group identity markers.

Peter: I think it would be fun to talk about that. Why don't we do- let's talk- for
   example my- the group process course.(0.6) I think it would be useful to have a
   group process theory,(0.7) and then even put more stress on the fact that group
   process is something that is created by the group.

Notice how he presents his idea in a jocular and colloquial way: "It
would be fun to talk about that." He also uses in-group markers and
pronouns to present his intention to change the subject. He appeals to the
others personally:

why don't we...

let's talk...

for example, my, the group process course

In summary, these members present ideas and introduce topics
through the use of solidarity and in-group identity markers: personal
examples, ideas formulated as needs and wishes, attributing one's ideas to
others, and jokes, humor and casualness. These linguistic strategies are
used by those members identified as having higher status in the
community.

## 5.2. Solidarity and deference strategies

How does this compare with lower ranking speakers? The following excerpts from the same meeting were from speakers with lower rank than Martin, Alain, Peter and George:

> Wendy: I think that it has to be coordinated between-(0.6) among individual classes, and not just- like like themes, I think it's great idea to have themes, like the first week covers (0.5) what we said, like philosophical concepts and stuff, (0.6) but then (0.7) I think at some point we need to exchange- all the teachers should exchange an outline more precisely, about what they're doing

In contrast to others', Wendy's utterance has very few pauses at tone unit boundaries and very few hesitation pauses. Shortened pauses at tone unit boundaries serve to shorten possible transition relevance places, thereby signaling to the others that they should withhold their bids for the floor. Furthermore, she frequently uses syntactic constructions implying obligation, necessity and requirements

> all the teachers *should* exchange an outline...
> it *has to* be coordinated...
> at some point we *need* to exchange...

In contrast to George's, Martin's and Peter's contributions, Wendy's uses the passive voice, impersonal verbs, and fewer personal pronouns and reference to personal needs and wishes. There is less use of solidarity and in-group markers, and an increase of impersonal, agentless sentences. The utterance is characterized by negative politeness strategies of impersonal verbs. Thus, we find the following impersonal constructions:

> *it's* great idea to have themes...
> *it* has to be coordinated between...

Later on, Robin, another participant of lower rank, makes a contribution:

> Robin: I had an idea about that. I was thinking if it was too- too- if we just said theory, that that probably would happen,(0.7) and that there might be something like-(0.7) I don't know, it could be difficult if people just like tried to talk about theory, y'know each time.(0.5) But if we were more specific,(0.6) like (.) we had started to suggest in deciding what we mean by theory, (0.5) which concepts, and also like a very (1.5) general and clear sort of essence, of what we really would like to get across during that time...

She, too, avoids implication and directness by using nominalizations and agent deletion:

*it* could be difficult...
if *people* just like tried to talk about theory
*there* might be something like...
and also like *a very general and clear sort of essence*
...like we had started to suggest *in deciding* what we mean by theory...

Karen, another lower ranking teacher, makes a contribution later on in the meeting, using the same negative politeness style of speaking:

> Karen: but I think it should also go like, the first thing in process theory that should be discussed probably isn't specific as that, but rather like philosophy or philosophical concepts...

Note, too, that similar to Wendy above, she uses modals expressing obligation and necessity without personalized agents or objects:

> I think it should also go, like, ...
> The first thing that should be discussed...

There thus seems to be a tendency among members of lower rank to use more negative politeness strategies, more deference and a more formal style of talking, while higher ranking members use solidarity strategies and in-group styles of speaking. To what is this difference due? In discussing language change, Labov (1966) discussed the connection between status and style of speech. He concluded that language change results from a pressure to use prestige forms or to avoid stigmatized forms. In our examples, however, there do not seem to be stigmatized or prestige markers, rather, we find lower ranking members using strategies which emphasize authority. That is, they seem to compensate their lower rank by using forms which give their utterances authority, influence and weight. They are negotiating their rank, attempting to increase their rhetorical power. The strategies found here reflect speakers' judgements about political and rhetorical power. The lower ranking members' style of speaking approximates the higher ranking attributes of authority and power, while higher ranking members use strategies of solidarity, informal speech styles, personal and in-group markers. Higher ranking speakers not only use solidarity to attend to the others' wants, but use these strategies to support the others' identity and position by "speaking their language." One sometimes witnesses this rhetorical device in political speeches, where politicians try to style their speech upon characteristics with which voters identify.

If we continue the Labovian principle that speaker's aspire to the speaking styles and strategies of higher ranking members, then we would expect lower ranking members to also use more solidarity and informal styles, to establish political effectiveness by an informal, personalized and in-group style of speaking. However, that is not the case. There is an asymmetry of speaking styles, not a tendency on the part of lower ranking members to use higher ranking forms. The situation is more akin to languages with *Sie/du*, *Vous/tu* distinctions: the higher ranking members have the power to use *du/tu* in conversation, non-reciprocally. Lower ranking members are still required to show deference. Even further, though, in contrast to Labov's premise, in the foregoing exchanges, we do not see stigmatized or prestige forms, but the use of various strategies in contesting of rank and power in conversation. *It is not the form istelf which is prestigious or stigmatized, it is their use in context.* Lower ranking members attempt to give their contributions more weight and authority. They speak faster, fearing that their contributions will be interrupted. Further, while the use of personalized markers such as "for me," "I feel," etc., show solidarity when used by higher ranking members, when used by lower ranking members, they show insecurity, hedging and minimizing one's opinions. This leads us to conclude that no speaking style itself has meaning, that is, no marker, style or strategy is inherently prestigious, stigmatized, higher ranking or lower raking. Rather, we must look at how strategies are used in each particular situation, taking into account speaker rank, network structure, and conversational setting.

## 6. Conclusion

This chapter has shown, using excerpts of multi-party talk, how politeness strategies, as defined by Brown and Levinson (1987), are really part of a larger strategy for maintaining the web of interpersonal relationship while simultaneously furthering the individual's standing in a group. Politic behavior is thus the careful balancing of individual self-assertion and self-presentation, and the need to avoid direct conflict and confrontation, that is, to attend to the other's positive self-image. Some of the strategies used to further speakers' own self-image while satisfying the other's positive face wants require that speakers shift their participation framework, that is, the relationship between the speaker and what is being said. By distancing oneself from their utterance, minimizing it, or even claiming their idea as similar to or as an extension of someone else's, speakers manage to avoid confrontation and minimize face threatening acts. We have seen in the data how speakers minimize the imposition of their face threat ("I just..."; "I only..."), defer to the other ("like you said," "...which is your idea"), exalt the other or the other's idea ("I think that's up to you guys"), claim one's idea as an extension of or similar to the others ("we could go a little bit further in the idea of Martin"), and, of course, go off record.

Strategies for going off record include stating one's idea as a matter of personal preference, subjective opinion or feeling. All of these strategies shift the speaker's participation status, i.e. the relationship between the speaker and what he or she says. As Shiffrin says, "opinions allow speakers to shield themselves from the truthfulness of the facts by focusing on their own stance toward what is being said (1990:245)." This shift in focus to what is being said also protects the speaker. Internal feelings and opinions are not generally available for inspection and are not subject to conditions of truthfulness. Opinions and feelings both *minimize* the force of one's statement ("this is just my personal feeling") and *amplify* it ("this is how I feel, and that's that). Whether stating something as a matter of opinion or feeling is done to minimize or amplify the force of what one says, its net result is that the other speaker will have a more difficult time refuting it. We will have more opportunities to observe and analyze this strategy in use in the next two chapters.

The network features depicting the social relationships of the organization reveal deeper insights about the interactions between the members. Specifically, cluster assignment, rank and degree of integration into the network play an important role in members' interaction. The patterns of social relationships in the organization are marked by two clusters, one extremely and one moderately dense. Interactions between members in a cluster are marked by a drop in politic linguistic behavior; members go on-record more, they are more direct, and conflict and confrontation is more likely to occur. Interaction between members of different clusters, or between people not socially connected, is marked by a degree of politic linguistic behavior, as in hesitation phenomena, hedging and indirectness.

The network structure revealed different interactional styles between high ranking and lower ranking members. Higher ranking members achieved political effectiveness by exploiting solidarity. They were more distant socially, yet used more solidarity politeness, personal forms of address and examples from their own experience, thus sounding more collegial and showing themselves to be equals. The strategy is based on interactants' mutual knowledge of speaking styles in relationships of minimal social distance. The leaders exploit this knowledge, knowing that, for instance, face threats indicate intimacy. The more formal the interaction, the more likely you are to be an outsider. The higher ranking members' interactional style was in marked contrast to the lower ranking members' tendency to use deference and formality strategies when speaking. This latter strategy seems to be an attempt to lend more authority and weight to the utterance, compensating lower rank, and thus attempting to achieve rhetorical and hence political effectiveness. In the next chapter, we will look more closely at political effectiveness and power in discourse, analyzing how speakers use discourse to achieve power and negotiate rank in interaction.

# Chapter Four: The Consensual View of Power in Discourse

Having looked at politeness strategies and politic verbal behavior, let us now look more closely at verbal interaction, specifically the ways in which speakers attempt to bid for power and negotiate rank in discourse. We will analyze instances of multi-party verbal interaction in order to see how power is vied for, assigned and maintained. Following our discussion in Chapter 1 about power, we will be analyzing power as consensual, as a role which is co-created by interactants. First, however, we shall discuss turn-taking and topics, aspects of discourse analysis which are necessary to our discussion of power.

## 1. Turn-taking

Analyzing how people talk to one another is an area of research within sociology and psychology as well as within linguistics. Bales (1950, 1970), for instance, researched group dynamics in small, task oriented groups and devised a method of analysis called *interaction process analysis*. His method is important because it is based on the principle of economy of speech; that is, the relative power or status of each member could be correlated with the types and amounts of verbal actions performed, i.e., giving orders, asking questions, offering advice, proposing solutions, etc. Individuals' actions are quantified and correlated with the variables of verbal activities, and then compared with the verbal activities of others in the group. His model is based on the economic principle that a turn is the currency of an exchange. The participant who talks longest or most frequently is in (momentary) possession of power. As Bales states,

> [t]he number of remarks is roughly equivalent to the time consumed. In a small group, time is like money or property. It is not distributed equally among members, but in a gradient that has some relation to the social status of the members....(The members) exercise power in the taking of time, though they may

not gain legitimate power. An increase in the amount of participation initiated by a given member may signal a bid for power (1973: 208-9).

Thus, merely speaking, or attempting to speak, can be an act of power, a competitive move. There are a variety of strategies and contexts which a speaker may employ in order to take a turn at talk.

This economic principle is found in the turn-taking model put forward by Sacks, Schegloff and Jefferson (1974), which is based on the notion that "one speaker speaks at a time." Since it appeared, the turn-taking model has been referred to so systematically by analysts of conversation that it can be considered a traditional model of conversational structure. The next section of this chapter will consider this model and note how interactional style can be observed through the turn-taking behavior of the participants. Some shortcomings of the model will be discussed, and alternative methods of analyzing interactional quality will be presented.

The turn-taking model begins with the simple and intuitive observation that talk appears orderly. People manage to converse in apparently orderly ways, and to shift from speaker to speaker, topic to topic, without too much friction and without an explicit set of social rules or conventions to follow. As speakers, however, we do not notice when talk is orderly, but when it is not. To notice disorder or chaos is to posit an implicit or underlying sense of order. That is, as speakers and listeners, we assume and expect that talk will be orderly and when it is not, we remedy the deviation or imbue it with social meaning.

Sacks et al. (1974) formulate a "rule," or rather a system, which attempts to make explicit the underlying order which ensures the smooth functioning of speaker switch in conversation. Following Schegloff (1968), their main premise is that in any conversation, one speaker primarily speaks at a time, and that turns are exchanged either through selection by the current speaker, or failing that, speakers compete for the floor through self-selection.[13] When a speaker self-selects, the turns are said to be locally controlled, that is, turn by turn. Furthermore, the majority of speaker switches occur at places in the talk which are distinctly marked prosodically, syntactically and semantically as *transition relevance places* (TRP). TRPs are frequently tone unit

---

[13] These findings may be found to be culturally limited. For instance, Japanese and African American English may present a completely different view of small group verbal interaction.

boundaries, where the intonation and pitch of the speaker drops off, where major syntactic units come to an end or close, and where ideas or information seem to be complete.

> If one examines empirical material to see where in an ongoing turn next speakers begin or try to begin next turns, one finds that such starts do not occur continuously over the developmental course of a turn, but discretely over its development. That is, possible transition-relevant places recur discretely in the course of a turn.... "next-turn starts"...occur at "possible completion points. These turn out to be "possible completion points" of sentences, clauses, phrases and one-word constructions and multiples thereof (Sacks, et al., 1974:34).

In conversation, overlapping speech occurs for as short a duration as possible. Overlapping speech is usually the result of a speaker self-selecting before the current speaker has finished his or her turn, or when one or more speaker self-selects after the current speaker has completed the turn. The observation that speaker switches proceed fluently suggests that there are cues speakers use associated with turn-taking. Duncan (1972, 1975), Duncan and Fiske (1977) and Duncan and Niederehe (1974) have discussed turn-yielding and turn-taking cues in dyadic conversations. According to Duncan, interruption occurs where there is an absence of turn-yielding signals (prosody, syntax, paralanguage, gesture) and smooth turn exchange occurs where such signals are present.

This brief outline of the turn-taking model shows that, similar to Bales' theory, talk is governed by an economic principle in which turns are the currency. Discourse revolves around the taking of turns and getting the floor; speakers vie for the floor, interrupt each other, raise topics, select themselves and others to speak based on the contest for turns. Sacks et al. recognize that

> [f]or socially organized activities, the presence of "turns" suggests an economy, with turns for something being valued, and with means for allocating them affecting their relative distribution, as they do in economies (1974:7-8).

Accordingly, one person speaks at a time and speakers manage to select themselves and others without too much overlapping or simultaneous speech. Interruptions, overlapping and simultaneous speech constitute dysfluent conversation and require repair. In fact, the authors state that repair is part of the turn-taking system. Speakers must use strategies that combine the desire to get the floor without jeopardizing too severely the entire interaction. Thus, interruptive behavior must simultaneously be redressed.

## 1.1. Overlapping speech

The difficulty in analyzing the interactional quality of a community or even of a small group through its turn-taking behaviors is that not all instances of overlapping speech are turn-competitive, nor are they interruptive. In fact, if we study casual conversation in groups of more than two people, we find that there are frequent attempts on the part of another participant to take a turn, resulting in overlapping speech into the current turn in progress. We would either have to consider small group behavior "deviant" or create ad hoc rules to account for the amount of overlapping speech in small groups. Yngve (1970) challenged the basic notion that overlapping speech was necessarily turn-competitive and thus a deviation from the norm by noting that there were many instances of non-competitive overlapping speech. He called these "back channel" responses, whereby listeners signal their attention to the current speaker. These may take the form of nonverbal responses such as eye gaze, smiling, nodding, or verbal cues such as "yeah," "mhmm" and "right." Duncan (1972) noted four types of back-channel behavior: verbalized signals like "yeah," "mhmm" and "right"; requests for clarification; brief restatements of part of the ongoing speaker's utterance; and sentence completion. These have also been called "accompaniment behavior" (Kendon, 1967) and "listener responses" (Dittman and Llewellyn, 1968). They are marked by an overt absence of the kind of prosody which usually accompanies turn-competitive bids, such as raised volume and pitch, brevity, repetition, etc.

The observation that not all overlaps or interruptions are turn-competitive led researchers like Ferguson (1977) to categorize types of overlapping speech. Ferguson identified four types of nonfluent speaker switches: simple interruptions, overlaps, butting-in interruptions and silent interruptions. French and Local (1986) examined the intonation structure of overlaps and found that while sometimes overlapping speech is directly competitive with the current speaker, at other times it is not. They state that determining the function of overlapping speech is best done by including the intonation contours of both the current speaker and the next speaker in the analysis. They found, for example, that thematic dissent alone, i.e., where the interrupter disagrees with the current speaker's topic, or interruptions at non TRPs alone cannot account for whether an interruption is turn-competitive or not. Rather, they suggest that increased volume and pitch are used by speakers and listeners to signal turn-competitive interruptions.

This focus on points of overlap in conversations is important because the concept that "one speaker speaks at a time" needs reexamination. It assumes that overlapping and simultaneous speech are points of dysfluency, dysfunctional communications or displays of dominance (cf. Zimmerman and West, 1975). Such an analysis cannot account for the amount and kinds of overlapping speech which occur in small groups. It also fails to consider non-white European American speech styles. Simultaneous speech, silence, back channel behavior are characteristic of other cultural speech styles. Additionally, when we look at small group behavior, these assumptions run into difficulty. As Edelsky (1981) has shown, in small groups of people, overlapping speech might be the norm. She shows that there are long stretches of talk where not only is overlapping speech the norm, but a current speaker cannot be identified: turns, floors, and even topics are held and developed collectively.

Another observation from our data concerns so-called back-channel behavior. In the text below, we see that Robin has the floor and is overlapped repeatedly at TRPs by what appears to be Martin's back-channel or turn-supportive behavior.

Robin: But if we were more specific,(0.6) like (.) we had started to be suggest in
    deciding what we mean by theory,(0.5) which concepts, and also like a very (1.5)
    general and clear sort of essence of what we really would like to get across
    during that      *time*, and then divide it up (0.7) (.) into like like f- what
Martin:               *mm*
Robin: Geor *ge was* saying, into these different (1.0) uh (0.5) channels, and so on,
Martin:    *mm*
Robin: that it wouldn't happen at all. Th*at*
Martin:                                  *mm*
Robin: quite the opposite would happen, that on- once *we start* working it *out,*
Martin:                                                *yeah*      *mhm*
Robin: because also there would be like (.6) exercises, and I was imagini *ng, (0.5)*
Martin:                                                                  *mhm*
Robin: instead of *talk about* how to do that within your *channel, (1.0)* ya know??
Martin:           *mhm mhm*                               *mhm mhm*

Robin: either can be very creative ???? {with it}\ we can- we can/ each person
Robin:    *could* also do *whatever* they want with that\ we could be very open also.
Martin:  *ja ja*           *ja ja*
Martin: Yeah. What you think, like my ideas for example, that on Wednesday, Can
    I {say something}?

Looking at the turn as it develops, we see that Martin's back-channel behavior actually precedes a bid for the floor. From the analysis of the longer stretch of text, it appears that Martin's back-channeling belonged to a superordinate verbal activity. Rather than appearing supportive, it appears impatient, possibly competitive. His back-channel responses increased in amount and frequency while Robin decreased the amount and frequency of her pauses, perhaps anticipating an interruption or sensing that Martin's back-channel behavior was a signal that he wanted to have the floor. We might conclude that this form of back-channel behavior is an indication of turn-taking readiness: it is a way to "share the floor" so to speak, without interrupting. To borrow an analogy from baseball, it is similar to being the "batter on deck," the next one up at the plate. In fact, this idea is lent support by Natale, Entin and Jaffe's (1979) study of interruptive behavior in which it was found that "a person's use of back-channel responses was significantly related to his or her overall rate of interruptions." Dittman and Llewellyn (1968) have also suggested that back-channel responses could be signals that a listener is preparing to take the floor.

Regardless of the interpretation of the overlapping speech above, the central point is that the most we can say about speech is whether or not it overlaps; describing it as a back-channel response, as interruptive, as turn-supportive or as turn-competitive are observer's *interpretations*. From the structure of a dyadic exchange alone we cannot extrapolate the function of overlapping speech. Furthermore, identifying the verbal behavior as turn-competitive or turn-supportive divides a speaker's behavior into units which may inaccurately portray the speaker's intent. That is, if, as Dittman and Llewellyn state, a speaker's back-channel behavior is related to his or her overall rate of interruption, why should we assume that the two phenomena are only coincidentally related? Could it not be that what the observer calls *back-channel* behavior is a turn-competitive strategy to get the floor? Our own terms and units of observation might obscure speakers' action.

How, then, can we define interruption? Could Martin's back-channel responses be interruptive? In fact, Ferguson (1977) even includes a "silent interruption" in her classification of interruptions. A silent interruption is one where a speaker's utterance is incomplete, and another speaker begins a next utterance. The example she gives is,

(A) It wasn't in ours actually it was a bloke, and um...
(B) But anybody who's a bit lazy I suppose, is it, that he used to pick on?

One further point of difficulty in this is brought to our attention by Watts (1991) who shows that speakers may interrupt a speaker selection. Speaker A selects speaker B, and before speaker B can take the floor, C self-selects. A's selection of B is interrupted. This adds a new aspect to the concept of interruption: *what* is being interrupted needs to be included in the research as well. B felt interrupted by C, even though B had not made a bid for or had the floor.

This discussion of overlapping speech demonstrates that it is necessary to look at conversation over a longer stretch of discourse, not just as a momentary dyad or exchange. The entire speech event, including participants and situation, needs to be taken into consideration. Speakers' own perceptions, as well as the progression of the turn over a long period of time, are crucial to an analysis of conversation. The turn-taking model has been, until now, an observer-oriented, rather than participant-oriented approach to conversation. In a study of speakers' perceptions of overlapping speech, Murray (1985) found that participants are more concerned with the notion of "making a point" than the technicalities of where, when and how their speech was overlapped. When asked, participants felt that

[b]eing superseded in speaking before making any point is clearly more serious a violation of speaking rights than being superseded before saying all one intended to say (1985:34).

Thus, the foundation of the structural model, that of economy of speech, is shaken: speakers are more related to the *quality* of contribution than the *quantity*. This suggests that topic and idea, i.e., *what* people say, might be a better tool of analysis of speakers' interactions than turn length and number.

## 2. Topics

Replacing the turn-taking model of conversational structure with a participant-oriented model takes into account what speakers say and their relationship to what they say. This necessitates a discussion of the term *topic*. The term has varying uses. *Topic* is universally recognized in the pre-theoretical sense as synonymous with "theme," or as Brown and Yule (1983:71) define it, as "what is being talked about." *Topic* is also used in transformational-generative grammar to identify a sentential constituent. This usage stems from the distinction of topics and comments in sentences (cf. Hockett, 1958), where topics are usually, though not always, the subjects of sentences, and comments are predicates. Another definition of topic has been put forward in the model of topic development in discourse by Keenan and Schieffelin (1976: 338) who define topic as "the proposition (or set of propositions) about which the speaker is either providing or requesting new information." This definition implies that what speakers say can be expressed by a proposition or set of propositions. It is an analysis which focuses on the state of information in discourse: are the speakers both informed of the referents in the text? How is given and new information differentiated in the text? How do speakers establish what the information is in a given topic?

A problem with the definition of topic as a set of propositions is that not everything said can be called informative. Propositions imply that communication is an exchange of information, but contributions are sometimes best understood by the function they serve, i.e., whether they ask a question, suggest a new idea, or support, contribute to or challenge the current speaker. A definition which equates discourse topic with a set of propositions about which the speaker is either providing or requesting new information, does not provide room for a speaker's intent, i.e. the speech act of the utterance. Brown and Yule's definition of discourse topic as "what is being talked about" includes speech acts, for speakers might describe a speech act when describing what is being talked about. For instance, speakers could give the following answers to the hypothetical question: What is being talked about?

1. She said X and then I said Y
2. We were talking about X.

3. I was trying to convince her that X.

4. Whether or not X.

Speakers can and do identify speech acts as topics. Topic as an analytical tool must therefore

refer not only to the subject of the ...conversation analysed...but also what was done with it. ...The discourse topic...invariably comprises the subject [i.e. topic] and the speech act associated with it (Bublitz, 1988:22).

If topics only referred to information about persons, objects, ideas, etc., then we would have difficulty accounting for Martin's comment to Laura, after she began to discuss the plan for the course: "It's up to you guys how you plan that. And I think that shouldn't be a democratic decision. " The surface semantic component of Martin's utterance alone does not yield a sound interpretation. If we concern ourselves only with propositions, we would be pressed to understand the remark only in terms of its ideational content, i.e. that course plans should not be democratic decisions. Understanding this utterance only in terms of its semantic component, shows it to be a tangential contribution to the discussion. A more cogent interpretation is yielded when we take into account not only the remark's ideational content, but the action it performs, as well as the social relationship to Laura which it implies.

## 2.1. Turns and topics

Our motivation for a topic-centered analysis of conversation is to find a unit of analysis with which participants identify. Speakers do in fact relate to what they say. They "are oriented towards ideas: they evaluate them, or present them neutrally; they express commitment to them, or distance from them" (Schiffrin, 1987: 27). Speakers do not speak in terms of turns, but in terms of "saying something." Furthermore, not every utterance is worth claiming; not every turn contains an idea that the speaker wants to bring forth. Speakers intend to say something, and, when asked, can explain their intentions. For instance, in multiparty conversations, sometimes a participant will bid for the floor unsuccessfully. Another participant might say:

A: Did you want to say something?

B: No, I was just agreeing with what he said.

This type of conversational interaction is not uncommon. It shows how ideas or topics are inextricably linked to turns and vice versa. Even types of overlapping speech might be differentiated according to whether or not and what kind of "topical contributions" they are. In the example of Martin's turn-competitive behavior above, which appeared to be turn-supportive, we could say that he was signaling his intention to table a topic. If we assume that in conversations speakers have things to say, then the currency of a conversation consists of ideas or statements rather than turns. Speakers have opinions, want to make contributions, tell narratives, raise objections, etc. How speakers do this requires rather sophisticated interactional strategies. Bringing in a new topic means shifting from the current topic. The dynamic whereby a speaker brings in, or raises, a new theme or topic I will refer to as introducing or raising a topic.[14]

Speakers shift from one topic to another frequently throughout any conversation. In fact, these shifts are often signaled through certain discourse markers such as "but," "and," "oh yeah," "by the way," "anyway," "that reminds me," "something else I wanted to say," etc. (cf. Shiffrin, 1987). Raising a topic is a complex activity, for it entails sub-strategies; one must not only bid for and get a turn to speak, but must also lead the talk in a new direction. Raising a topic successfully necessitates ending or shifting away from the current one, and also having the new topic ratified and picked up by other participants. Thus analyzing topics and topic raising includes an analysis of speakers' effectiveness, for it forces us to look at the entire interaction, including the subsequent actions of both the topic raiser and the other participants.

Topics cannot tell us much in isolation. They are developed over the course of a conversation by one or several speakers. We therefore need to analyze longer stretches of text if we are to make a valid interpretation of the situation. We cannot know, for instance, whether or not a topic is successfully introduced by looking at the immediate environment alone. Very often a topic is not taken up straight away by other participants, but will be raised again later in the discourse, either by the same or a different participant. Thus, raising a topic has meaning only when we consider the subsequent activities of the participants. Is the topic picked up by someone else immediately or later on? Is reference made or credit given to the one who raised the topic? Is it raised again by someone else

---

[14] I use these two terms interchangeably to avoid confusion with the concept of topic raising in transformational-generative grammar.

who claims it for him or herself? Is it ignored altogether? We must be careful, however, not to use the concept of topic within an economic framework, for topics can also be constructed or shared by a number of participants. Ideas have a tendency to "float," so to speak, from one participant to another, especially in a meeting. We see, over the course of an hour, for example, that the same idea is raised in a number of different contexts, and then finally agreed upon or rejected. It is sometimes difficult to find out who is responsible for introducing the idea.

I would like to suggest that through topics speakers not only take the floor, but also make a contribution to the group, claim a position, and become what I call a "resource person." The resource person is the one who has momentary access to co-creating or shaping the direction of the group and its policies. The one whose topic is accepted by others is the one who is momentarily creating and interpreting the experiences of the group, creating an impression that, if accepted, the group will project.[15] It is a position of political leadership if we define leadership as the ability to bring in ideas and create policy. In order to raise a topic, however, some minimal requirements need to be met.

## 3. Topic ratification and refusal

In accordance with Bublitz's (1988) definition of discourse topic as the combination of topic subject (*what* is being talked about) plus an accompanying speech act (the speaker's intent), we need to differentiate two aspects of topic raising in discourse. When a speaker's topic is ratified by other speakers, its status as a topic of conversation is accepted by exhibiting their willingness to argue about it, even if the content (i.e., the *idea* expressed within the topic) is rejected. In other words, the act of arguing about an idea, or even rejecting an idea, is still considered topic ratification because the topic becomes a subject of conversation. A case of valid topic rejection happens when the speaker's intent to put forth a discourse topic as a matter of discussion is not taken up at all. This type of topic non-ratification takes the form of interlocutors ignoring, silencing, minimizing or refusing to develop the speaker's contribution further. Thus, the two elements of discourse topic - the speech act (the

---

[15]   cf. Mannheim, 1968:240 ff.

speaker's intent) and the discourse subject (the idea, or what is being talked about) - lead to different modes of topic ratification or rejection. There are, however, face threats inherent in both a rejection of the speech act and of the subject. How speakers deal with the insecurity inherent in raising a topic will be the subject of study in the following pages.

Saying something in a multi-party interaction is not a simple procedure. Speakers do not just have things to say, but do things with what they say. Speakers

> take action using discourse topics; one can play around with them, as it were, one can handle them in a certain way and one can, of course, make use of them in order to steer the conversation and to influence one's interlocutor (Bublitz, 1988:40).

Topics need to be introduced into the conversation by speakers. They are developed, created, introduced, shifted, closed and used by speakers to assert rank, maintain face and challenge the face of others. These activities of topics in discourse contribute a structural and interactional component to a model of discourse. Speakers assert their rank and signal their relationships to other speakers through topical actions. Topics contain not only ideas, but information about the speakers' commitment to the ideas, and their relationship to other speakers. The speaker who manages to develop his or her topic of choice and to mobilize the others to ratify it, increases his or her rank in that network.

Raising a topic is a complex procedure which consists of sub-steps and linguistic and relational strategies. It would fall outside the scope of this study to outline the entire procedure involved,[16] yet a number of elementary steps can be outlined. Raising a topic entails, first of all, talking.[17] Once the speaker has the turn, he or she must either close or shift away from the current topic with the consent of the other participants. One of the immediate constraints on speakers who introduce a new topic is to make their topic coherent and continuous, that is,

> listeners will not accept...referents that they cannot identify in terms of general knowledge, prior discourse or present context. Speakers make an effort as well to

---

[16]  cf. Bublitz, 1988, for a comprehensive analysis of topics and topical actions in conversation.

[17]  I shall avoid using the term "floor" as synonymous with "talking" as the definition of floor is, according to Edelsky (1981), the "psychological time/space within which things are said and done." Topics are introduced onto the floor and one or several speakers can develop the topic, and hence said to be "on the floor."

insure that listeners can identify what or whom they are talking about (Keenan and Schieffelin, 1976:338).

The new topic must be in some way continuous with the foregoing one. If it represents a completely new theme, participants must be able to differentiate new from given information in the topic, and be provided with markers signifying that the foregoing topic is being closed or shifted. Thus, the speaker raising the new topic needs to receive consent from the other speakers on two accounts. First, he or she must receive the consent of understanding and comprehension from the other speakers that the topic shift meets the requirements of discourse cohesion. Second, the speaker must redress the face threat implicit in shifting the topic away from the current one.

### 3.1. Raising a new topic as an FTA

Raising a new topic or shifting away from the current one is a threat to the speaker who raised the last topic and to the speakers engaged in developing it. Because of the dual aspect of topic and topic raising, i.e. the speech act and the topic subject, raising a new topic while speakers are still engaged in developing the current one has a double face threat inherent in it: if the central idea has not yet been brought across, introducing a topic is a face threat because the new topic leaves, shifts away from or rejects the current subject of conversation. Secondly, raising a new topic threatens the intent of the current speaker, i.e. his or her act of developing a topic. Thus, discourse markers signaling a new topic must serve at least two functions: they mark the transition from old to new topic and redress the implicit face threats (cf. Schiffrin, 1987). Speakers redress the face threat of raising a new topic by embedding it in polite formulae, in a conciliatory fashion, and by hedging and tempering their remarks with markers such as "well," "by the way," "anyway," "but," etc. Our data show speakers raising new topics through strategies that "soften the blow" of revising, neglecting or rejecting a fellow speaker's topic. For instance, in TR01, Alain raises a new topic after Martin gives his views. He attempts to alleviate the implicit face threat to Martin by crediting his own topic to Martin: "I think we should go a little further in the idea of Martin."

Presenting one's own ideas as an extension or reformulation of the previous speaker's topic is a strategy we have already seen in the data. Speakers have an intuitive awareness that when they attempt to shift the topic away from the current one, it could be construed as a threat or challenge to the speaker or speakers engaged in the current topic. Notice below Martin's polite strategies as he attempts to shift the topic away from the route Laura has chosen:

> Martin: I c- I can- I can tell you- I ca- Can I say something? I th- I think my need is uh (0.9)- would be (1.2) to hear (0.7) what the people plan to do, (.) more than like discuss (1.0) how you- I think that's up to you guys, how you plan that. (1.0) And I think that shouldn't be a democratic decision.

Martin "softens the blow" by using the polite strategy of deferring to and strengthening Laura's decision-making capacities: "I think that's up to you guys, how you plan that."

## 3.2. Bidding for power and speaker insecurity

Introducing a new topic or shifting away from the current one is not only an implicit FTA to the speaker(s) engaged in the current topic, but also entails a risk to the positive self-image of the one who raises the topic. Raising or introducing a new topic requires the consent and ratification of the others; the speaker's topic could be ignored, rejected or silenced. Additionally, even if the topic is ratified, that is, becomes a matter of discussion, the idea or subject of the topic may be rejected or disputed. The possibility that one's topic or its idea may not be ratified by or receive the consent of others makes speakers insecure. Contributing to a discussion may backfire and leave speakers feeling less powerful than if they had said nothing at all. The rank one gains by introducing a topic that others ratify is proportionate to the risk one takes in introducing it.

The need for ratification and speakers' insecurity when raising a topic is observable in the way they prompt other participants for a response to their new contribution or idea. An overly long pause at a turn relevance place after a topic has been introduced or shifted, at what could be considered an utterance completion, is an uncomfortable moment for the speaker. A speaker who does not receive a satisfactory ratification response may fill in the silence with prompts: repeating or reformulating the proposed topic, or explicitly requesting a response.

Alain: We could do something like that, like, uh (0.9) we could go a little bit
further in the idea of Martin, (0.6) give certain themes (0.5) per week, (0.5) that
should be treated around uh (1.3) that uh (0.5) classes should be arranged those
themes. (1.1) Something like that.
Laura: mhmm mhmm.
   1.3

Alain presents his idea, and at a turn relevance place, there is a 1.1
second pause. He then prompts the others ("Something like that") which
receives only "mhm" from another member, and again is followed by a
1.3 second pause. We could say that both the speech act (the intent of
contributing) and the discourse topic (his idea) were not enthusiastically
greeted by the others; he was thus left in a vulnerable position. Topic
ratification is not a discrete event. As we all know, the enthusiasm or lack
thereof with which our topics are met range from great excitement to
mild interest to complete disregard. Furthermore, because of the dual
aspects of topics, the intended speech act (the speaker's intent to
contribute) may be ratified, that is, become a topic of conversation, but
the idea may be rejected. For instance, a speaker may raise a topic which
is ratified, that is, becomes a topic of conversation, but the idea may be
disputed or met with a tepid response. In such a case, the speaker may
prompt, explicitly or indirectly, the other speakers to consider the idea
further, as Sylvia does below.

Sylvia: You know, (2.4) one idea of mine, (.) was uh (1.2) to like hire a band.
   1.7
Wendy: That'd be great.
Kim: That's an *interesting idea.*
Sylvia:      *Do you think that'd be good?* One of my neighbors, y'know,
Monika, she sings in a band.

At the surface semantic component of the above interaction, Sylvia's
bid was ratified by the others. Wendy replies, "that'd be great," while
Kim says, "that's an interesting idea." However, the interturn pause of 1.7
seconds indicates that while the topic is ratified, the content is not
immediately taken up by the others. Thus, Sylvia prompts the others for
more acknowledgment: "Do you think that'd be good?"

Social constraints in North American/Western European cultures
require listeners to positively acknowledge speakers' contributions,
through back channel responses, such as "mmhmm", "yeah", "right",
"really", "yeah", etc. However, it is not always apparent whether or not
one's idea was genuinely acknowledged, or whether the listener was

providing the perfunctory, required response. We are therefore forced to consider extralinguistic cues in addition to listener responses, as listener responses are, so-to-speak, requirements of the situations. Interturn pauses are very good cues, for, as we have seen above, even when the listener grants the bid a comment such as, "that'd be great," the speakers respond to the pause which precedes the comment, rather than to the comment itself. Above, Sylvia prompts the others for more acknowledgment even after having received the two responses. Thus, it appears that she treated her listener's responses as perfunctory, but not the long interturn pause of 1.7 seconds. Her prompt for a response in addition to the two responses implies that she treated the pause as a more genuine indication of her listener's sentiments.

How do we know when an interturn pause is too long? It is not possible to define a long pause, for interturn pauses vary from situation to situation. In a multi-party interaction where turns are locally managed, interturn pauses will be relatively short. In a mediated discussion in a formal setting, interturn pauses may be longer. As these pauses are relative from situation to situation, we can only define a long interturn pause by comparing it to an average interturn pause for the speech situations we have recorded here. On the average, in our data, in fluent[18] multi-party interaction interturn pauses last approximately 0.8 seconds.

In the previous example, Alain's topic is met by an initial interturn pause of 1.1 seconds, followed by his prompt, "something like that," and then a second interturn pause of 1.3 seconds. He is in a more vulnerable position than Sylvia, for while her topic was ratified, though its idea was not enthusiastically responded to, his topic was hardly ratified, with the exception of one perfunctory back channel response, "mhmm mhmm," by Laura. In another example, below, Kim's topic is met with a 5.0 second interturn pause. She too prompts the others directly for a response, "whadya guys think? should we do it?" This, too, is met with a half second silence. Finally, she begins to redress the situation by directly inquiring whether or not the others oppose her idea.

> Kim: I like that id- I like that idea. I like your idea for the last th- thing, (.) and
> your idea for the whole community.

---

[18] I am differentiating fluent interaction from interaction characterized by conflict, for in situations where speakers are in conflict with one another, there may be longer interturn pauses.

5.0
Kim: Whadya guys think? Should we do it? (0.5) Is anyone against it? Or is--
In the examples we have seen so far, the speakers introduce a topic
and either reformulate or reiterate it when they do not received a
sufficiently prompt or enthusiastic ratification:
y'know?
something like that
or, they prompt the others for a response with direct questions:
Do you think that'd be good?
Whadya guys think?
In the first example, Sylvia uses the discourse marker "y'know" as a
prompt for listener participation. As Schiffrin (1987:290) says, "'y'know'
marks the speaker as an information provider, but *one whose successful
fulfillment of that role is contingent upon hearer attention*" [italics mine].
  Another strategy speakers sometimes use to preserve their positive
face is to either directly interpret or predict the lack of response. Above,
Kim employed this strategy when, after 5.0 seconds of silence, she asked
the others: "is anyone against it?" This strategy is akin to "going on the
defensive." Speakers in the insecure position of waiting for the others to
acknowledge their act of contributing, or the merit of the contribution
itself may directly challenge the other's silence, and, by so doing, reverse
the face threat, putting the others in the position of having to go
on-record about their silence. In other words, instead of reformulating or
prompting others as a way to preserve her positive face, Kim directly
quizzes the others on their silence and threatens their negative face.
Below, in an exchange between Wendy and Laura, Wendy demonstrates
another form of this strategy:
Wendy: I mean, (3.4) theoretically, we would have a free room to offer.(1.5) I
  mean, I- you would probably- wouldn't want to, but I would offer my room.(1.5)
  I mean, I'm paying for it, and I'm not living in it.(1.8) But (.) that's really up to
  you.
  4.6
Laura: yeah\
  0.7
Wendy: You think about it.
Wendy's response, "You think about it," follows almost 5 seconds of
intraturn pauses at turn relevant positions, and an interturn pause of 4.6.
seconds. This is an extraordinarily long interpause turn for a dyadic
exchange. Receiving only the minimal, "yeah," and that after a 4.6.

second pause, suggests that both the speech act and the discourse subject are not being ratified. Finally, she opts out of the topic by saying, "you think about it." As we have seen, speakers who receive little or no ratification on their topic have two choices, one which threatens their own positive face, and the other which threatens the negative face of the hearer. The speaker may continue to insist on his or her topic, or may withdraw the bid for ratification. Here, Wendy chooses the latter. Yet it is clear that her positive face has been threatened by Laura's minimal response. Her method of withdrawing is to acknowledge Laura's silence and support it, doing a turn-around. In other words, Wendy's face is threatened by not receiving a prompt response, and so she attempts to repair her face by telling Laura that her silence is an accepted, perhaps even an expected response, making it seem that Wendy is *requesting* the silence from Laura. A last strategy we will see shortly, is for a speaker to withdraw a topic whose content is not being ratified. When no amount of prompting, reformulation or reiteration brings forth a desired acknowledgment of the idea, the speaker is obligated to abandon the attempt and let the listener off the hook.

To summarize, when a speaker raises a topic, he or she will employ discourse markers, explicit requests for confirmation, summaries or reiterations in order to receive the necessary response which ratifies his or her topic, both the speech act and the discourse topic. Ratification of topic means ratification of the speaker's role as information provider or resource person. In our analysis, we will not equate the introducing or raising of a new topic with power, rank or role of resource person. Rather, raising a new topic is a bid for the role of momentary resource person which can only be obtained through the consent and ratification of the other participants. So far we have been focusing on the speaker's strategies for getting a topic ratified. What about listener's strategies for refusing or rejecting a topic, or disputing and rejecting its accompanying idea? Our data have shown that silence, as conveyed in interturn pauses, is used to withhold ratification of the speech act. But what about situations where speakers are directly requested to respond to the speech act, or situations where the speech act is ratified, but speakers are put in the position of having to go on record rejecting the topic idea?

## 3.3. Rejecting a discourse topic

The following excerpt, TR02, is a meeting of four members of the same cluster. The activity centered speech concerns plans for a party for course participants. Notice the freedom with which turns are taken and overlap occurs, relative to the larger and more formal meetings, TR01 and TR04. The meeting takes place over dinner in a restaurant. Some of the long pauses are due to the activities of eating. In the excerpt below, Laura raises the topic of having a talent show during the party.

> Laura: I'd like to handle that because I had an idea. And I'd like to ask you guys
> what's your idea about that. (0.5) I would really like to do something we thought
> of last year, and that is, I would really like to have (.) (0.6) a variety show, (.)
> talent show, party, (0.9) in which- in which we charge a little bit to make a little
> bit of money, (0.6) and everybody does acts. (.) And there's judges, and people
> get prizes, and it's--
> Sylvia: Everybody? That's a little-
> Kim: I don't like the idea.
> Wendy: I don't like it either.
> Kim: [laughter]
> Wendy: [laughter]
> Laura: You don't have to- to- wait a mi- you don't have to- not everybody, (.) you
> know,  people who want to. You know, it could be really funny or humorous.

Laura's topic is ratified; that is, the other speakers immediately respond to her bid. The idea, however, is rejected outright. We can sense Laura's insecurity about the topic by her introduction, using five different hedges before presenting the idea itself:

> I had an idea...
> I'd like to ask you guys...
> What's your idea about that...
> I would really like to do something we thought of last year and that is...
> I would really like to have...

These hedges indicate her need for the others' support for her idea. Laura's uncertainty is also indicated in the way she describes her idea using three synonyms: variety show, talent show and party. She tries to get her idea across by telling the others that it is something she would "really like to do." This method, as we discussed in the last chapter, of stating something as a personal feeling, can minimize the force of one's statement ("this is just my personal feeling") or amplify it ("this is how I feel, and that's that"). Here, it seems that Laura is amplifying her appeal: "I really want to do it."

Though the topic was ratified by the other speakers in their rejection of it, there was a lack of immediate response, indicated by the pauses at transition relevant places during her introduction: "I would really like to have (.) a (0.6) variety show, (.) talent show, party. (0.9)" At the tend of the tone unit, variety show, there is a slight pause. This would be the appropriate place for responses, remarks or comments from the others. Receiving none, she proceeds. She reiterates and provides synonyms for her idea in the hope that the reformulation will call forth agreement from the others. This point highlights the speaker's vulnerability in introducing a topic, for its success depends on the others' reaction. We have seen that in the event of a topic not being ratified, whether the speech act or the discourse topic, the speaker can attempt to elicit responses from the others by offering them openings for their response.

Laura's topic is ratified, but the idea is not. Sylvia, Kim and Wendy repudiate the idea in different ways. Goodwin and Goodwin (1990:94) discuss different types of refusals in conflict talk. One way of accounting for a refusal is for the speaker to emphasize that he is "acting purely in terms of his own desires," for instance, above, when Wendy and Kim both say, "I don't like it." Goodwin and Goodwin (1990:94) cite research (M.H. Goodwin, 1980b, 1988) which shows that "accounts of this type are frequently used by boys attempting to display their relative power or status vis-a-vis each other." Other ways to account for a refusal are "found in the task activities of girls which rely on legitimate demands of the activity in progress, rather than status claims of participants (Goodwin and Goodwin, 1990:94)." In our data, we do not find that these different accounts for refusals correspond to differences in sex. Rather, we find that speakers alternate between refusals on the grounds of personal feeling or as legitimate demands in order to minimize the severity of the face threat, as we shall see. Sylvia's objection minimizes the face threat of rejecting Laura's discourse topic. It is an off record objection in that she does not object to the idea, but to an aspect of it. This is a negative politeness strategy to redress the implicit FTA, whereas the others veto it directly, with no redressive action: "I don't like the idea."

Speakers reject, dispute or disagree with others' topics and ideas through a variety of strategies: but (used to contrast), yeah, also, (used to connect the previous utterance to one that follows), and so (used to summarize the previous argument). The following strategies were found in meetings TR01 and TR04:

ja, for example...
but *actually* we could *also* have like uh, a, an *s' gaege argumaent als das*
   (opposing argument from that one)
yeah, *but* there's a way to do that...
I think it's great idea to have themes, *but* then--
*but* maybe now we can like do that...
*so* what you think, that like you said that, like the
*yeah*, what you think like my ideas, for example
but I think it should *also* go like...

Speakers can also reject topics or raise new ones by including them in the new argument or by presenting them in terms of their personal desires:

I think *my* need is er would be...
I like the idea of themes, but...
I think it should also go like...
But there's a way to do that...
But maybe now we can like do that..
So what you think? Like *you* said....
OK let's go back to the curriculum. Let's...I'd like to go back to the curriculum.

There are also frequent occurrences of the discourse marker *like*. It marks the following text as an approximation, a vague guess, not an exact definition. It is a way of going off record by encoding vagueness and ambiguity. What the speaker says is not to be taken as a matter of fact. It is not the thing itself, but like (similar to) it.

At the larger meetings not once did a speaker say directly to another, "I don't like it," as Wendy and Kim said above. It is clearly a sign of intimacy and of situation that speakers forego the need to minimize face threats. Situation constrains speakers' relationships. Though many of the speakers at the meeting are intimate friends, the situation requires the use of negative politeness forms, rather than the language of positive politeness. The norm at large meetings is to use language which maintains the negative face-wants of participants. By manipulating the forms of polite language usage and speech situation, speakers are able to create metaphorical and non-linguistic meanings. In other words, if a speaker shifts repertoires, and uses the language of positive politeness in a situation requiring negative politeness forms, he or she creates meanings. An example of this is found in TR01 when Martin appeals to his personal need ("My need would be"). His shift in repertoires signals solidarity to the others, and that what he is saying needs to be considered carefully.

Going back to TR02, Wendy's and Kim's responses to Laura's idea are in keeping with the language of positive politeness. What strategies does Laura employ to negotiate the rejection of her idea?

> Laura: You don't have to- to- wait a mi- you don't have to- not everybody. (.) Ya
> know,  people who want to, ya know. It could be really funny or humorous.

Her frequent self-corrections are attempts to respond to both objections at once: Sylvia's question ("everyone?") and Kim and Wendy's flat refusal. The self-corrections are coupled with appeals to the others: "wait, ya know, you don't have to...". Laura uses the discourse marker *y'know* frequently in the passage. Schiffrin (1987:294) defines *y'know* as "an information state marker: it marks transitions to meta-knowledge about shared knowledge." *Y'know* also has interactional functions. In the passage, Laura uses *y'know* to engage the active support of her listeners. Her attempts, however, do not work, and her topic is flatly refused. After a few more appeals, she drops her idea and the meeting moves on to another topic.

## 3.4. Withdrawing a discourse topic

There is a marked contrast in the way Laura's idea has been received by the others and the way Sylvia's idea was responded to earlier in the chapter:

> Sylvia: You know, (2.4) one idea of mine, (.) was uh (1.2) to like hire a band.
>     1.7
> Wendy: That'd be great.
> Kim: That's an interesting idea.

Though the others ratify Sylvia's topic, i.e., their responses indicate that they agree to discuss the discourse topic, the pause, as well as the intonation contours of their responses, betray hesitation towards the idea. However, Sylvia continues to present the idea by explaining why she had it. The other participants, Wendy and Laura, do not pursue it directly, but digress onto a related topic.

Sylvia: You know,(2.4) one idea of mine,(.) was uh (1.2) to like hire a band.
  1.7
Wendy: That'd be great.
Kim: That's an *interesting idea.*
Sylvia:                   *Do you think* that'd be good? *(.) One*
Wendy:                                          *Mhmm.*
Sylvia: of my neighbors, y'know Monika, she sings in a band.
  1.4
Laura: I think I know who she *is.*
Wendy:                            *Did* you recommend her to call us for English
Wendy: lessons? (.) Is th *at Monika?*
Sylvia:                         *Yeah. (1.3)* She like- she's lazy. She's (0.7) getting bored

Digression, like content shift, is a way of avoiding having to oppose a discourse topic. If speakers cannot agree with an idea, they must find some way to continue the conversation.

> [A]rgument would be severely constricted if it had to come to an abrupt halt every time someone made a statement that could not be disputed. Instead, by shifting topic participants are able to continue an opposition sequence without denying the validity of what the other has just said (Goodwin and Goodwin, 1990:98).

The digression continues for few minutes, and then Kim tries to get the others to go back to the topic at hand: Sylvia's idea to hire a band.

Kim: Whadya guys think? Should we do it? (0.5) Is anyone against it? Or *is-*
Sylvia:                                                          *I think*
Sylvia: they charge normally eight hundred francs. Is that too much,(1.1) for a
   band?    0.5
Wendy: I'm not sure about the band idea,(0.5) *myself.*
Laura:                                   *I don't like it.*
Sylvia: mhmm\(0.6) (.) Let's not do it.
Wendy: (0.9) I like it.(0.9) I like it in princip- in like- im prinzip.(.) *(.) But*
Sylvia:                                                          *mhm*
Wendy: I feel like-(1.3) it's like the beginning of the intensive course. People
   wanna get to know ea-(0.6) I think--

Wendy's hesitant objection, displaying a negative politeness strategy, "I'm not sure about the band idea", is contrasted sharply to Laura's: "I don't like it." Wendy rejects Sylvia's topic by putting it in terms of her personal desires, "I'm not sure about the band idea.....myself." This use of a personal feeling or desire, as we have seen, can either be used to minimize or amplify one's statement. Here, it seems that Wendy is not asserting her status by personalizing her argument, but minimizing the imposition of her refusal. We see this is in the way she follows on by saying, "I like it *im prinzip* (in principle), but...." . Introducing ideas or topics as a personal wish or desire can also be used to ensure that one's counterargument cannot be repudiated. Wendy hedges her opinion about Sylvia's suggestion: "I'm not so sure about it...myself." Her objection falls outside the scope of fact and opinion and is thus difficult to attack. Further, it preserves Sylvia's negative face (as well as Wendy's) by minimizing the threat of the imposition or disagreement. The minimization lies in the fact that what she is saying is "just" her own feeling, i.e., not an objective criticism of or opinion about Sylvia's idea. How does Sylvia take this? She capitulates:

Kim: Whadya guys think? Should we do it?(0.5) Is anyone against it? *Or is-*
Sylvia:                                                                      *I think* they
   charge normally eight hundred francs. Is that too much? (1.1) For a band?
   0.5
Wendy: I'm not sure about the band idea,(0.5) myself.
Laura: I don't like it.
Sylvia: Mhmm.(0.6) Let's not do it.

Sylvia takes back her idea: "Let's not do it." Wendy, however, does not accept this at face value, but continues to state her objections, even though, to all intents and purposes, Sylvia withdrew the topic from the floor.

Sylvia: Mhmm (0.6) (.) Let's not do it.
Wendy (0.9) I like it.(0.9) I like it in princip- in like- im prinzip.(.) *(.)*
Sylvia:                                                              *mhm*
Wendy: But I feel like-(1.3) it's like the beginning of the intensive course, people
   wanna get to know ea-(0.6) I think--

Why is this? It might be that Sylvia's submission is perfunctory. We would expect her to defend her idea, to argue for it more, as Laura had done earlier, "wait a minute ya know, it could be really funny or humorous." Furthermore, Sylvia's tone is matter of fact. We are thus led to believe that Sylvia's statement "Let's not do it" is a perfunctory submission. She could be withdrawing because she wants to avoid further confrontation, already having picked up on the lack of enthusiasm. One line later, however, she re-establishes her arguments. In fact the argument continues for another five minutes.

Sylvia: But we can like open different rooms, you know.(0.6) Certain people get to
   know each other much better in move*ment. They dance together.*
Wendy:                                      *So why not just have music?(0.8)* That
   way-(0.7) I mean- why (0.5) have like a-(0.6) *(0.8) so- in a small*

Laura: *Somehow, it seems* like -
Wendy: roo- like the room's not so big. *It seems like-*
Sylvia: *They're not-(0.5)* th-
Sylvia: th- they don't have to play tha*t loud,(.) you know.*
Kim: *What kind of music* do they play?
Sylvia: I think it's like old jazz stuff, and uh (1.7) I don't know exa*ctly, really.*
Kim: *Old jazz is*
Kim: hard to dance to really, you know.
Sylvia: No- I don't know- but- they make music {to dance to}. I don't know, (0.6) I
  would have to like get a tape from them.
Kim: mmh

Sylvia counters each objection by Wendy with a counter-argument.
Notice Wendy's diplomacy. Though she does not like the idea, she
engages in a discussion about it. Kim employs a different strategy: she
asks what kind of music they play. Kim is not personalizing her
argument, but trying to legitimize her rejection, finding objective grounds
upon which to reject the proposal. As Sylvia sees that her idea is about to
be vetoed, she abandons her strategy:

Sylvia: I don't know, I just- I personally would like it, you know. I would like to
  be ????, and I also think it would be fun, *(.) and* stuff, *(1.1)* and uh (.): -
Kim: *yeah*
Wendy: *mhmm*
  2.5
Wendy: mhmh
  2.0
Kim: Well that costs eight hundred francs.
Laura: I would rather just not spend the money,(1.9) ya know.(0.9) Cause (.)
  people (1.2) I feel like (0.6) parties are (0.7) so anyhow difficult, and like (0.6)
  they're so individualistic. And (0.9) you never know how people feel, and (1.2)

Sylvia abandons her strategy of legitimizing the request using the
issues of cost, loudness, general desirability of a band, and instead
appeals on the grounds of her personal desires. Once again, we have the
strategy of attempting to get one's idea ratified by appealing to personal
desires. And, once again, we can interpret this as a strategy to either
minimize or amplify the appeal. In this case, Sylvia's personal desire
amplifies the imposition. Rather than discuss the pros and cons of the
idea, Sylvia asks the others to approve of her idea. This puts Wendy and
Kim, the main opponents of the argument, in the position of having to
veto Sylvia's direct wishes. This changes the participation framework of
the argument; Kim and Wendy are in danger of rejecting Sylvia, not just

her idea, for Sylvia has changed her own relationship to what she says. She now identifies with her idea. This strategy threatens to stall the argument. After Sylvia expresses her personal wishes, Kim's and Wendy's arguments are reduced. There is an extremely long intraturn pause of 2.5 seconds, followed by "mhm" and then another pause of 2.0 seconds.

Kim retreats to the business argument, disregarding the change in participation framework, and objects to the cost of the band. Laura, too, uses the legitimate issues of money, available room space and number of people to argue against the idea. Interestingly enough the speaker's strategy of changing the participation framework does not necessarily insure that the others ratify this change; the other participants can and do ignore the change. Their lack of acknowledgment of the change in participation framework helps them avoid going on record rejecting Sylvia's idea, but it deadlocks the argument. Sylvia's attempt to provide an argument of personal desire was not picked up by the others. It appears that one cannot "win" an argument established on someone's personal wishes. Rejecting someone's personal wishes, as we have already seen, runs a greater risk of impinging on the person's face wants. Thus the argument continues, but it seems deadlocked. For every argument, there is a counter-argument.

Wendy: I'm not- I'm mixed about it, really mixed about *it*.
Kim:                                                    *I'm mixed too.*
   1.0
Wendy: I think it's a good idea, and I'm not positive.
   1.3

Wendy and Kim cannot directly veto the idea. To what is Wendy's hesitancy and diplomacy attributable? Her diplomacy and hesitancy stand in contrast to her earlier veto to Laura, just a few minutes before:

Laura: I would really like to have a variety show, talent show, party...
Kim: I don't like the idea.
Wendy: I don't like it either.
Kim: [laughter]
Wendy: [laughter]

Wendy's hesitation cannot therefore be attributed to a personal characteristic, nor to the nature of the meeting. Rather, we must conclude that there is greater social distance between her and Sylvia. The members cannot risk the imposition of a direct veto. The meeting is at a stalemate not only because Wendy and Kim cannot accept Sylvia's idea, but because they cannot reject it. At a point like this, the only option is for Sylvia herself to withdraw the idea.

This situation highlights an important feature of this small group discussion. It appears that the person who raises a topic or idea has an obligation to withdraw or terminate his or her argument if it is not accepted after sufficient discussion. That is, the one who raises an idea or topic is not only in a vulnerable position, as we stated above, but is in a position to forestall decisions and stalemate a meeting. Raising a topic can thus be an imposition, a face threatening act that impinges upon the negative face wants of the others not to go on record by rejecting the idea. The one who introduces the discourse topic must preserve the negative face of the others by withdrawing his or her idea in order to prevent the others from having to reject it on record, and thus commit an FTA. For instance, in the current meeting, the other participants are in a difficult situation; they are either forced to commit an FTA by not accepting Sylvia's idea, or are forced to prolong the meeting indefinitely, as is the case here. Thus, there is an obligation for speakers to adjust their behavior to the indirect and deniable communications of other speakers. Sylvia is under an obligation to terminate her own idea because of the uncertainty and ambivalence found in the others' long pauses, intonation, prosody, and continued argument, even though they have indicated interest thematically.

This might be a feature particular to small task groups, where plans and programs are forged. In contrast to groups where issues are decided by voting procedures, in small groups such as this one, it is frequently the obligation of the person who raised the discourse topic to withdraw it if he or she sees that it is not being accepted. When the network ties between the participants are insufficiently close to bear direct rejection, the one who imposes by bringing in the topic is obligated to give the others a way out, an opening to reject without directly rejecting. This function is usually served by institutional mechanisms, such as voting, where a discourse topic can be shelved without any single individual having to take responsibility for the action.

At this particular meeting, Sylvia fails to withdraw or terminate her own idea. She continues arguing and, in a sense, violates the others' negative face-wants by forcing them towards an on record rejection. The discussion cannot move forward or backward, and simply draws to a standstill:

> Wendy: I'm not- I'm mixed about it, really mixed abou*t it.*
> Kim:  .                                            *I'm mixed too.*
>    1.0
> Wendy: I think it's a good idea, and I'm not positive.
>    1.3

Finally, after almost ten minutes of discussion, Sylvia withdraws her topic by postponing the decision to a later date:

> Sylvia: So why don't we think about it? We don't have to decide it now.
> Wendy: OK.

She does not withdraw the idea, but gives the others an opportunity to leave it undecided. This then is a way out of the deadlock. Sylvia does not withdraw the discourse topic officially, but implicitly, by postponing the final decision to an indefinite future time.

## 4. Conclusion

### 4.1. Topic analysis and power

The empirical data have demonstrated the usefulness of considering ideas and topics, in addition to turns, as units of analysis. Raising a topic or bringing in an idea necessarily includes turn-taking mechanisms. Thus, an analysis of the speaker's ideas or topics can bring to light interactional strategies speakers use beyond those for getting and maintaining the floor. We have seen, for example, how speakers contest their rank and exert power by bringing in their ideas, rejecting others' ideas, disagreeing and arguing.

The types of interactions we have been observing are occurrences of negotiation and competition for rank, status-roles and power. In its most simple form, the exertion of power takes the form, in Western European/North American cultures, of being the speaker or central resource person. Power is displayed in the ability to exert an influence on others, to interpret events and have those interpretations accepted, to perpetuate one's role, to define others' roles, and to do all this without too severely harming the fabric of interpersonal relationships. Thus, examples of power being exerted in discourse would include: bidding for the floor successfully, talking and holding the floor for lengthy periods of time, being listened to and agreed with by others when saying something, having others follow a suggestion or advice, etc. And once again, as rank and power are culturally relative, the exertion of power and rank in one culture will be done according to its own specific set of values and ideology.

This analysis has revealed a number of interesting features around the raising of a topic. First, a topic consists of both the speech act (the intent of saying something) and the discourse topic (the idea). The speaker who raises a topic is thus twofold insecure: first the speech act must be ratified, then, if ratified, the discourse topic could be rejected, ridiculed or dismissed. Thus, raising a topic is a bid for the position of resource person, a position of power, yet is also a display of vulnerability, for the topic raiser is dependent upon the acknowledgment and support of others. If either the speech act of raising a topic is not ratified, or the discourse topic is rejected after debate, the speaker who raised the topic will prompt the others for a response, reformulate, reiterate or supply synonyms for the idea in the hope for further ratification or discourse topic development. In the case that a topic is ratified, but the discourse topic (idea) is not being supported, the speaker may be forced to abandon his or her own discourse topic. In certain types of speech situation, such as the small task-oriented groups we are looking at, the one who raises a discourse topic has an obligation to withdraw it from the floor if, after sufficient arguing, it is still not accepted. Thus, the one trying to develop a discourse topic can stalemate a meeting, or compel the other participants to go on record by rejecting the idea. This leads us to conclude that speakers are expected to attend to the unintended or, as Labov and Fanshel (1977) call it, the "deniable" level of communication. The success of participants' strategies to indirectly express disagreement, hostility or rejection depends upon the other participants' implicit agreement to attend to those strategies. In other words, deniable, indirect and ambiguous communication only works when all parties tacitly agree to that system of communication.

There are a number of interesting repercussions to these findings. For one, they show that, unlike other analyses of interactional structure, particularly that of interruption and turn-taking, power does not reside in any single strategy or in any single speaker. That is, there is not one inherently effective strategy speakers use, nor is any one person in the interaction in sole possession of power. Power is negotiated over the course of an entire interaction. For instance, even in a case where a speaker's discourse topic is rejected, as in TR02, where Sylvia's idea is rejected by the others, Sylvia's strategy for negotiating this rejection is to reverse the face threat and force the others to go on record as rejecting her proposal. Speakers exploit the rich encoding potential of language to convey social meanings, specifically, to negotiate and contest power.

Therefore, if power cannot be said to reside in one speaker or in one particular verbal strategy, then the concepts of weak and strong in discourse and social structures need to be re-examined. Studies in which certain verbal behaviors are deemed dominant or submissive, for example, equating interruptive verbal behavior with dominance, as Zimmermann and West (1975) do, overlook the entirety of the interaction. Speakers' actions after an interruption, over the course of the entire interaction, must be included in the analysis. Similarly, other studies of power in discourse, for instance, in therapy or doctor-patient situations, need to reevaluate the *a priori* assumption that a lower institutional rank automatically means less rhetorical power or less local rank.

## 4.2. Power as consensual

In our discussion on power in Chapter 1, we said power was "political and consensual," and defined it as the

> ability to interpret the events and issues of a time and place, and have these interpretations accepted. It is not only a property invested in an individual, but a self-image or role which is contested, vied for and negotiated in discourse and which needs ratification from others (p. 14).

This is a definition of power as the manipulation of roles, roles being synonymous with self-images. The roles that we take on, inhabit, so to speak, and assign ourselves and others, depend on the consensus of those to whom we present them. Saks and Krupat have found that while researchers

> claim that the relationship between doctor and patient is really characterized by a struggle for power in which doctors attempt to maintain control over patients by using jargon, pulling rank, and controlling information available to patients ...

[p]atients [also] use a variety of "doctor management" techniques from subtle strategies of influence to deliberately refusing to take their medication (1988:132).

Thus, consensual power means that the self-images we create are a jointly developed construction of social identity. Identity is a collective process. One's identity is created not only by the individual, but by the audience which receives, acknowledges and responds to the identification. One's identity is contingent upon it being acknowledged and ratified by those to whom one presents it. Therefore, the audience members, the ratifiers, share in the process of power. Even dictators will be overthrown if the self-images they seek to project and preserve are no longer ratified by the people of their country, as events in Eastern Europe from 1989-1991 have demonstrated. In fact, a

hierarchy is...a collaborative achievement, accomplished as much through the actions of the subordinate part (who actively demonstrates his willingness to change his behavior at the suggestion of the other) as through those of the dominant party. From such a perspective a hierarchy is an activity, a phenomenon accomplished by participants through a range of specific of specific interactive work (and thus something to be explicated through concrete analysis of the details of their talk), rather than a description of a static feature of the social organization of a group (Goodwin and Goodwin, 1990:113).

This, then, is what we mean when we say power is political and consensual; it is a process, not a static characteristic or description of a person or social structure. Power is always in a state of dynamic flux, being collaboratively created throughout discourse by all participants. If interactants vie for power in discourse, manipulate roles or self images, and seek the ratification of these roles by the other participants, then discourse must run the risk of developing into conflict. In fact, all discourse transpires against a backdrop of latent conflict. Conflict is potential in all interactions, if we understand interaction as the presentation of self-images, for as we have now clearly seen, taking on a role is a competitive move which automatically assigns the other participants a role as well. We therefore cannot speak of power in discourse without addressing the latent, and sometimes overt conflict in discourse as well. The next chapter will go deeply into conflict and competition in discourse, and show how conflict is latent in participant footing, competition and rivalry in discourse, and how speakers manage conflict when it does surface.

# Chapter Five: Conflict and Competition in Discourse

## 1. The nature of conflict

The term *conflict* refers to a wide range of human behavior. There are countless forms of conflict and often little agreement as to whether or not conflict may be present. It is not uncommon for interactants to deny or minimize conflict when it is present, and even to argue about whether and what kind of conflict they are involved in. Boulding has defined *conflict*

> as a situation of competition in which the parties are *aware* of the incompatibility of potential future positions and in which each party *wishes* to occupy a position that is incompatible with the wishes of the other [italics his] (1962:5).

This definition describes conflict, as we have in the last chapter, as a contest for roles and positions. He includes, however, that the participants must be aware of the incompatibility of the desired role. He acknowledges the difficulty of using the terms *aware* and *wishes*, for these words, he says, "are laden with philosophical dynamite." Awareness is difficult to determine. As we stated above, participants are fond of denying or minimizing conflicts. If we deny the existence of conflict, or minimize it out of fear of reprisal or fear of losing face, yet, when pressed, admit that we are minimizing it, can we be said to be aware of the conflict or not? Thus, Boulding is not referring to the participant's awareness of conflict, but to the awareness of the *position* or *role* that the opponent occupies.

It is possible, therefore, and even common, for opponents, individuals or nations, to deny the existence of conflict, and be aware of the positions or role which their opponent occupies. For instance, one or even both members of the conflict situation can admit to feeling victimized and treated unfairly by the other. They will describe their behavior in the conflict as a defense against the unfair accusations or attack of the other. This is a form of denying conflict. They insist that they are not in a conflict with the other, but merely trying to right an unjust situation in which they are being victimized. In fact, discourse, as we have been viewing it, is an interactional process in which participants continually define their position vis-a-vis the other and jockey for rank with one another. Thus, conflict is latent in all discourse, but only seldom is it raised to the level of consciousness. In fact, the entire premise of politic behavior, negative and positive politeness strategies, is based on the assumption that participants do everything in their power to avoid outright confrontation and to keep the interaction flowing in a smooth and harmonious way.

Our empirical data show that speakers may be in conflict with one another, and can even disagree or dispute without communicating *about* the conflict. As Bavelas, Rogers and Millar state,

[m]ost interpersonal conflict is verbal, not physical; the conflict is the argument itself. ...In linguistic terms, interpersonal conflict is a speech event; it is performative in that saying equals doing. The argument, quarrel, insults, or disagreement are the conflict. In other words, people do not relate, then talk; rather, they relate in talk (1985:9).

In some cases, interactants will go to great lengths to avoid a direct confrontation, and in other situations, it appears that interactants are quite comfortable with conflict talk, bald face threatening acts and other forms of direct confrontation. In fact, as we intuitively know from our own experiences, the presence of conflict may be an indication of the close social distance between interactants. As Grimshaw says,

the absence of visible conflict [does] not necessarily mean that apparent harmony [is] real. ...Interactants motivated to maintain a relationship and concerned that it was not a strong one would avoid conflict-while individuals confident about a relationship would more comfortably engage one another in dispute (1990:300).

## 1.1. Constraints against conflict

The denial of conflict cannot be due solely to a lack of awareness or refusal to acknowledge reality. There are very necessary and important reasons to minimize, deny or refute the existence of conflict. The chief reason is fear of reprisals, for in our society there are numerous constraints against individuals directly disagreeing and voicing opposition, particularly if one's conflict partner is of a higher rank (cf. Grimshaw, 1990; Bublitz, 1988; Brown and Levinson, 1978). The constraints are cultural, social and situational. There are widely different views to conflict and public displays of affect across cultures. Even within cultures, there are widely divergent sub-cultural attitudes. Black and white Americans differ widely in their style and method of conflict, as has been noted elsewhere (Kochman, 1981). Gender differences in conflict have also been researched extensively (cf. Tannen, 1984, 1987).

There are also social and situational constraints on conflict. In white, North American/Western European cultures, many people people feel that conflict is something done within the privacy of one's own home. "Dirty linen" is not to be aired in public. Furthermore, settings and scenes constrain conflict. The church, classroom, store, or someone else's home may be considered inappropriate settings for conflict. Power and rank differentials are also serious constraints on conflict talk. Students do not, as a rule, pick fights with teachers; children are not supposed to talk back to their parents; an employee, fearing for his or her job, will not argue with the boss, etc. These constraints are very real and are often manipulated by those in the more powerful position. Finally, interactants are constrained in their conflict talk by the presence of what Goffman (1981) calls "non-ratifed overhearers," i.e. audience members witnessing the conflict. Thus, in the data, we have many examples of members disagreeing, but few examples of members addressing the conflict explicitly. The few examples that are present are limited to exchanges between close friends in intercluster situations.

## 1.2. Forms of conflict

There are different forms of conflict that the observer may notice. According to Grimshaw,

conflict talk, like all discourse, can be: (1) direct or indirect; (2) "cool" or "passionate"; (3) based on facts or opinions (though each may appear in the garb of each other); (4) procedurally formal or informal; (5) based on appeals to morality or to codified norms (including law) or both; (6) based on appeals to reason or threats of force, etc. (1990:294).

In our data, we find that conflict is rarely raised to a level of explicitness between participants in meetings and discussions. In other words, the conflict we do find is "cool," rather than "passionate." There is only one instance where the participants actually have an overt conflict, and the only reason we know that is that one of the participants apologizes to the other.

The data are organized into the following forms of conflict: conflict of relational roles, managing overt conflict, and competition and rivalry in discourse. These categories may overlap. For instance, rivalry and competition may become overt. I am not suggesting that overt and covert conflict are mutually exclusive, but separating overt from covert conflict shows how discourse consists of background struggles for power and rank and a foreground concern with avoiding direct confrontation. I wish to show how participants use discourse to negotiate roles, contest power and rank, and compete with one another while keeping direct conflict and confrontation to a minimum.

Before we turn to the data, however, it is important to mention one last observation about conflict. Though commonsense tells us that we win and lose fights and conflicts, it is rarely, if ever, the case that verbal disputes are won or lost. Even though we talk about winning, losing, and beating the opponent, we all know that silencing an opponent does not necessarily mean that we have won the fight. As Grimshaw notes,

> ...there are "winners" and "losers" in conflict talk but "winning" can be ambiguous and "victories" can be Pyrrhic, partial, inconsequential, temporary, or false. Second, superficial appearances are often misleading; this is true both in the sense that hidden agendas may be more important to participants than "official" ones...and in that conflicts that appear to be over may not be at all (1990:304).

Even in the case of national and world wars, where there are designated winners and losers, both sides of the conflict suffer great casualties, financial loss and psychological damage. As Boulding says, in regard to class conflict,

> ...conflict is not like two dogs struggling for a bone in which, if one gets more, the other gets less. It is much more like the evolutionary conflict of species, in which temporary advantages often lead to ultimate defeat (1962:207).

## 2. Conflict of relationship roles

### 2.1. Social identities and social organization

Many sociolinguistic studies of discourse have analyzed the way social identities construct, constrain and effect talk (Labov, 1966, 1972a, 1972b; Bernstein, 1971; Blom and Gumperz, 1972; Lakoff, 1973; Brown and Levinson, 1978, 1987; Trudgill, 1978;). Sex, race, socio-economic status, power, etc, have an important effect on the way in which talk is organized. These studies have dealt with how social identities and roles constitute the talk of the moment. Yet in our analysis we are taking a consensual view of power and roles: though participants have permanent social identities, much of their social identity is constructed by contesting their social roles from moment to moment through the vehicle of discourse. The goals for this study of conflict come close to the objectives of Goodwin and Goodwin who are interested in

> the way in which the talk of the moment constitutes those who are present to it (i.e., how what is said in a given turn can make relevant particular social identitites). A participant building an appropriate oppositional move must attend not only to the action that is being opposed, but also to...how those present are being positioned vis-a-vis each other (1990: 85).

In other words, it is not so much the social roles we take with us into an interaction which shape the talk of the moment, rather, it is the talk of the moment that shapes our social identities and that of others. Conflict strategies therefore are attempts to reshape how we are aligned to each other and attempts to "strategically alter the social organization of the moment (Goodwin and Goodwin, 1990:85-86)."

### 2.2. Vying for rank and leadership

A typical type of conflict over relationship roles is seen in children's play. Children frequently fight over who gets to go first, who gets to play with the big truck, who gets to stay on the swing longest, etc. The only difference between how children vie for power and leadership and how adults do it is in how open and obvious the struggle is. Adults vie for leadership and power every bit as much as children do; they just use more sophisticated, embedded devices. An example of conflict as a disagreement over roles is seen below. In TR01, the discussion concerning curriculum is coming to a close. The teachers have reached an agreement to set a fixed week-by-week agenda for the classes to follow. Martin has been more or less the de facto leader of the meeting, making the most contributions and bringing the meeting to a decision. In terms of local rank, Martin has a higher rank in the eyes of the community members than does Alain (see p. 45), though both have almost similar institutional rank. Towards the end, the following exchange takes place.

> Alain: I have a suggestion. (0.7) Why not uh (0.5) now make uh (.) that agenda,
> (0.6)    *with* uh (.) what we'll- with the the uh *(.)* themes, (.) and uh (0.7)
> Martin:  *yuh*                                           *yuh*
> Alain: we go to it and discuss it.
>   0.5
> Laura: Mhm.
> Martin: Yeah, let's do i*t. That- that's what we're doing.*
> Kim:                    *OK, let's do it.*
> Laura: Let's try it.
> Klaus: Right.
> Alain: Let's get started - let's get together.(0.6) What- to what the uh (0.5) themes gonna be.

This exchange can be seen as a challenge from Alain to Martin over the role of discussion leader, and hence over local rank. Alain's suggestion, "Let's make an agenda," is a bid for momentary leadership, and thereby challenges the role of leader and coordinator that Martin has taken on. Martin counters Alain's challenge, "That's what we're doing," and in so doing, rejects Alain's bid for leadership and its implicit criticism of Martin's role and capabilities therein. Martin defends his role by changing the participation framework. He makes a metalinguistic comment, "that's what we're doing," questioning Alain's capacity to follow what the group is doing, and asserting his own leadership by telling Alain what the group is doing. In effect, Martin counterbids Alain's attempt to control the parameters of the momentary activity. His comment, "that's what we're doing," shows that he has not let go of the leadership position. It could be construed as a derogatory comment, belittling Alain's perception, although it is off record enough to prevent a direct face threat.

Competition for leadership is one of the classic types of conflict over roles and positions. Goodwin and Goodwin (1990), in an analysis of a boy's sling shot battle, show how the talk preceding the actual battle already contains the conflict over roles. In the exchange Michael and Huey are identified as team leaders, and they are just about to choose their teams.

1. Michael: All right who's on your side Huey.
2. Huey: It's quarter after four and I'm not
3.      ready to go yet.
4.      I'm not going till four thirty.

The exchange shows how the talk that occurs is about the upcoming conflict, but also has conflict already present. The boys are jockeying for leadership. In line 1, Michael's question to Huey addresses him as a leader in the sling shot activity: he has the power to choose sides. Yet in lines 2-4, Huey not only acknowledges the role given to him by Michael, but also refuses to perform the action according to the time frame set up by Michael. In other words, he has "jumped a level," so to speak, and bids for a position of power over Michael by contesting when the activity will occur. Huey attempts to put the activity of sling shot battle under his control, not Michael's.

In terms of roles and role assignment, we can see that Michael's initial question addressed Huey as co-leader, but was also an attempt to take control. His question was more like an order, telling Huey to choose sides. Huey's response challenged that assignment, and re-assigned the roles. Michael's question, "who's on your side Huey" is more than a question; it is an attempt to control the timing and structure of the activity. Huey's lack of compliance, "I'm not ready to go yet" indicates that he will not be put into the role of the compliant one. He therefore counter-bids (and wins) the stab at leadership. (Goodwin and Goodwin, 1990:95)

This example is interesting for it looks at conflict at two levels: the overt conflict is or will be the slingshot battle, but the covert conflict is the struggle over leadership between Michael and Huey. The two examples of conflict we have been looking at are not overt; they arise over the contest for roles in a given and momentary relationship. The self-image that an individual presents is one that stands in a complementary relationship to others' self-images. For instance, a self-image of a therapist, i.e. one who is able to interpret the actions of others, necessitates another with the self-image of a client. For instance Alain's suggestion was a bid for the role of coordinator, a role that Martin had had until then. Alain's definition of himself impinges upon the self-image Martin had been projecting. It is thus role competitive. Michael's suggestion that Huey pick his team was a bid to control the timing and thus the activity of the sling shot battle.

## 2.3. Metaphorical switching

Let us now look at another type of conflict over role and role assignment. The interaction is from TR03, a Thanksgiving party with approximately seven friends present. Wendy interrupts Larry's narrative. This is a conflict between friends, although they are not in the same cluster. Wendy has slightly more rank in the organization, both institutional rank, as a member of longer standing, and local rank, being perceived by others with higher regard. Larry is telling a story of his parents meeting a mutual friend for the first time. He is discussing the discrepancy between his friend's public behavior towards his parents, and what his friend had told him in private.

Larry: When (.) like they- they met him he said they were so great and I thought
(1.0)    *"Am I just crazy?"*
Wendy: *No it's just that now* you have to stand up for yourself without using him
as a third party\ *he's like ?????\ [laugh]*
Larry:            *Right, right, but but-* during the conversation I thought (0.5)
"Am I just crazy?"
Wendy: Oh.

What is the conflict here? Wendy challenges Larry directly by refuting his interpretations and conclusions of his own story. She re-interprets his behavior and understanding of his own experience and thereby makes a metaphorical shift in style; she uses therapeutic discourse in a party situation. This metaphorical shift is a change in participant status. She redefines her self-image; she is not just listening to his narrative as a fellow party member, but is interpreting his behavior. This redefinition of her own role also redefines his role, for it assigns him a new position, that of client to her therapist. Concretely, the metaphorical shift we are speaking of is that from informal, casual discourse to therapeutic discourse in a situation where this is not appropriate. Therapeutic discourse refers to the style of speaking in which one's personal experiences and interpretations are called into question. In most discourse, disagreement and argument are limited to information to which both parties have access. Personal feelings, experiences and interpretations are typically outside the realm of dispute. Yet in the therapeutic situation, the therapist has the right to call the client's own feelings, subjective responses and interpretations into question. It is this difference that distinguishes the therapeutic situation from others (cf. Labov and Fanshel, 1977; Lakoff, 1989).

This example also shows us how ubiquitous conflict is. In any discourse, each individual's contribution can be seen as claiming a self-image which automatically defines the other's. This is not limited to therapeutic situations. Our presentation of a given self-image necessitates a definition of the participants involved. There is conflict inherent in all interpersonal relationships; each individual's self-image poses a threat to the others present. Yet it is only where there is open disagreement, refusal or rejection of the definitions we assign to ourselves and others that we speak of conflict. This idea has been discussed at length by Bateson (1951) and Watzlawick et al. (1967) who

were particularly interested in the "command" (Bateson, 1951) or "relationship" (Watzlawick, et al., 1967) level of a message, rather than in its content. That is, they assumed that any message not only conveys information but seeks to define or redefine the nature of the interactants' relationship (Bavelas, et al., 1985:18).

In the example above, Larry appears to go along with Wendy's definition ("Right, right"), but continues to emphasize his own interpretation ("but, but..."). Thus, the two are in conflict with each other in that they are contesting the relationship roles through the struggle of defining Larry's experience.

Another type of metaphorical shift involves speakers changing the situation or activity by shifting content. In the example of the slingshot activity between Michael and Huey, we saw how the boys were vying for leadership through their attempts to control the timing of the slingshot activity. After Huey disputes Michael's claim for the leadership, how does Michael take Huey's refusal? Does he simply accept this assignment? What are his strategies for getting leadership?

1. Michael: All right who's on your side Huey.
2. Huey: It's quarter after four and I'm not
3.          ready to go yet.
4.          I'm not going till four thirty.
5. Michael: Well get in here and get them papers off that couch *before-*
7. Huey:                                              *I did already.*

Having lost the intitial bid to tell Huey when to pick his side, Michael is left with a challenge. What does he do? He switches the talk to a completely different setting. Though the talk still contains the underlying leadership struggle, it makes a content and setting shift, to household chores. What is the use of content shifts in argument? As we have discussed, roles are specific to situational features. Thus, in different situations, actors have different roles. In the street, Huey and Michael are both team leaders, but in the domain of household activity, they are brothers. Thus, the shift of domains is equal to a shift of roles. The strategy Michael invokes is to assert his leadership by evoking another situation.

> Michael abruptly shifts the content from sling-shot teams to household chores, and in so doing, automatically changes the participant roles from team-leaders to brothers...[T]he shift to talk about household duties, and the new social identities for participants thus invoked, provides a way for Michael to construct an appropriate next move within the emerging opposition in sequence (Goodwin and Goodwin, 1990:99).

Thus, the use of topic in the analysis of talk is lent support by this example. We have seen how topic is a better description of the framework of talk than turns. Topic contains an important strategic element in conflict talk:

> [B]y virtue of its ability to invoke alternative situated activity systems, topic provides parties to a conversation with resources for rapidly changing how they are aligned to each other, and the activities that are relevant at the moment (Goodwin and Goodwin, 1990: 111-112).

## 3. Overt conflict

### 3.1. Managing face threats

Let us turn to overt or explicit conflicts, where the parties identify a conflict, discuss it, and try to do something to remedy the state of conflict. These situations usually occur between participants of minimal social distance, such as family members, partners, husbands and wives, or intimate friends. In the following example, two members of a dense cluster, Wendy and Laura, come into conflict during a meeting with one other person present, Kim. Wendy had been renting a room at Laura's house and had just decided to move out, though she was still paying rent. In the midst of the discussion about finding housing for financial aid students, Wendy suggests that her room in Laura's house be used to house a scholarship student. The following conflict ensues:

> Wendy: I mean, (3.4) theoretically, we would have a free room to offer. (1.5) I
> mean I- you would probably- wouldn't want to, but I would offer my room. (1.5)
> I mean I'm paying for it, and I'm not living in it. (1.8) But (.) that's really up to
> you. 4.6
> Laura: Yeah.
>    0.7
> Wendy:You think about it.

Wendy must have some awareness of committing a face threat here, for her frequent pauses, self-corrections, and use of the discourse marker "I mean" to qualify her statement, point to uncertainty about what she is saying.

> *I mean*, theoretically....
> *I mean*, you would, probably wouldn't want to...
> *I mean*, I'm paying for it....

Schiffrin (1987) considers the discourse marker "I mean" a function which paraphrases speaker's intentions, and which also serves metalinguistic and metacommunicative purposes. Schiffrin distinguishes metalinguistic from metacommunicative functions in that the former refers to ideas, and the latter to

> the speakers' communicative act. ...It is the narrow meta-linguistic focus of *I mean*
> which allows it to be a modifier of speakers' ideas, and the broader
> meta-communicative, interpretive focus of *I mean* which allows it to be a modifier
> of speakers' intentions (1987:304).

Wendy uses "I mean" to metacommunicate about her coming intent: "I mean" precedes her remarks, suggesting that she needs to clarify her intentions. "I mean" is also used as an attempt to withdraw from a conflict. It can be seen as an offer of submission and repair. The speaker uses "I mean" to modify his or her position, withdrawing from any conflict or competitiveness which his or her statement may have exhibited.

The extremely long intraturn pause of 4.6 seconds following Wendy's initial suggestion shows Laura's reaction to Wendy's statement. Undoubtedly reading Laura's displeasure into the long pause, Wendy

attempts further repair by telling her, "You think about it." Exactly what
kind of face-threatening situation is this? It is not quite the same as the
above challenges between Larry and Wendy, and between Alain and
Martin. Whereas those interactions challenged the relationship roles and
assignments, the conflict here is more complex. Wendy suggests a
possible solution to the problem. Her suggestion, appropriate to the
discussion of financial aid, presents a self-image of generosity. Laura
hesitates responding to the suggestion, since it entails an intrusion into
her privacy. Laura's face has been threatened by Wendy's suggestion; by
not responding positively to the suggestion, Laura runs the risk of going
on record refusing room and board to an indigent student. On the other
hand, her negative face was threatened: something of hers was offered
without her approval or consent. In the analysis of the implicit conflicts,
we saw how one's self-image necessarily assigns the other to a
complementary role: therapist-client, leader-participant, sling-shot battle
leader and follower. Here the challenge is to pick up the role
symmetrically. Wendy's offer puts Laura on the spot, so to speak, to
show the same self-image by being equally generous. Since Wendy's
offer was couched in conditionals and hedges, when Laura attempts to
object, Wendy claims that her request was off record. Notice the
difficulty Laura has in objecting; she is constrained by the potential loss
of face implicit in refusing to be equally as generous.

Laura: Yeah, (0.6) I mean- I feel like you- you- just cause you're paying for i- I
mean- I feel like (.)--
Wendy:That's why I'm saying it's up to you.
Laura: Yeah.
0.6
Wendy:I'm saying that, theoretically, if *we both wanted to-*
Kim:                                        *It doesn't sound like you said it.*

The argument is about the conflict itself; they are not so much arguing
over whether or not to offer the room, but about what Wendy has said.
The discussion is primarily concerned with the "on recordness" or "off
recordness" of the request. Laura takes issue with the fact that Wendy
offered her room. Wendy denies that she offered it, i.e., she claims that it
was off record, which it was, in the sense that it was conventionally
indirect, couched in conditionals, self-corrections, and hedges. The
frequent use of metalinguistic remarks highlights the fact that the conflict
is the argument itself:

That's why I'm *saying* it's up to you.
I'm *saying* that, theoretically, if we both wanted to--
It doesn't sound like you *said* it.

Laura challenges Wendy's claim that the statement was off record, and insists on her own interpretation of Wendy's statement. She holds Wendy responsible for what she perceives as Wendy's intentions. In other words, Laura equates the intention of the remark with the effect it produced. Goffman says that,

> [r]egardless of whether a person intends to take a line, he will find that he has done so in effect. The other participants will assume that he has more or less willfully taken a stand, so that if he is to deal with their response to him he must take into consideration the impression they have possibly formed of him (1967:5).

Participants hold each other to the effect that is created by an utterance, and do not, as a rule, trust what people say they intended with an utterance. This can be seen in arguments, for example, where participants contradict each other's statements, paraphrase what the other has said, and fight about the way in which the other is fighting. Initially, the conflict concerned Wendy and Laura. Suddenly Kim comes in and takes Laura's side.

Wendy: I'm saying that, theoretically, if *we both wanted to-*
Kim:                                  *It doesn't sound like you said it.*
Wendy: (to Kim) What's the matter? What?
Kim: I don't know, I had a- I had a reaction, when you said that also, a
    fe*eling thing.*
Wendy:     *Did I say* something wrong?
Laura: It was a little s- weird.
Kim: Yeah.

Kim's perceptions support Laura's; she interpreted Wendy's remarks in the same manner as Laura. This creates a coalition between Kim and Laura against Wendy. They both hold Wendy responsible for the effect of her remarks, despite her spoken intention to the contrary. The alliance results in an offered apology from Wendy.

Wendy: I'm sorry. (0.6) I'm being- I'm sorry. I have to say- let me take it back.
    (0.7) I take it back.(1.5) I'm just (0.5) putting it out as an option, and I feel like
    it's completely up to you.(.) I feel li*ke (0.6)* I
Laura:                                  *mhm\*
Wendy: wouldn't do it. I don't think,(1.9)     *(0.6) I don't* think I would do it.
Laura:                                  *[suppressed laugh]*
Wendy: I mean I think it would be really hard for me. (0.8) But I just put it out as
    an option, and if I said it in any other way, I- I just thought of it, just now. (.)

And I blurted it out, and I'm s- I wanna apologize Laura. I take all pressure off
you, cause I don't think I would do it.

## 3.2. Speech act as face threat

Why is an apology called for? Why did Laura not respond when
Wendy gave up her idea? Wendy does not apologize for the *idea*, but for
the *utterance* itself. The conflict is around the *speech act* that Wendy
committed: offering a room in Laura's apartment without first consulting
Laura. The *content* of the utterance, i.e., whether or not someone should
rent the room, is beside the point. That would be a matter of fact,
something to voice one's opinions about, to discuss and debate. Wendy
apologizes for her speech act by explaining her intentions: "I just put it
out as an option". She even gives Laura a way to save face by admitting
that she, too, would not do it. The conflict had two parts: first, the speech
act was an affront to Laura's negative face in that it impinged upon her
wants. It did not accord her the opportunity to refuse or object to what
was essentially something of her own being offered. Second, her positive
face was threatened in that if she objected, her self-image as a generous
and considerate person would be damaged.

These analyses of conflict situations show that there are different types
of conflict and that conflict is found at different levels of an utterance.
*What* a person says can be face threatening, and what a person *intends*
with a statement, or the speech act itself can be face threatening, as in
this case between Wendy and Laura. There is also a third aspect to
conflict. One's face is threatened by the fact that one is in the unfortunate
position to be face-threatened. This is one of the uses of the term *face* in
the Japanese culture: your honor has been defamed by the injustice done
to you. This was part of the face threat in TR03 where Wendy challenged
Larry. His face was threatened because Wendy challenged him publicly,
thereby showing him to be vulnerable. Conflict carries meaning. Just as
the presence of face threats may signal closeness or intimacy, or fights
might be a "sign" of love,[19] so too can the fact that one's face is
threatened indicate being in an inferior role. Thus, conflict is avoided,

---

[19]  Couples have been known to brag, "We've had our first fight," indicating new
levels of intimacy and closeness.

denied and expressed through conventionally indirect discourse out of the desire to avoid the face threat implicit in being caught in conflict.

Going back to the example, Wendy's apology only addresses Laura's negative face. Her positive face has to be addressed as well. That is, she needs the opportunity to redeem herself, to re-establish her positive self-image as someone with a generous and altruistic nature. Thus she redresses her positive face by declaring her good intentions towards the students:

Laura: I mean, I thought of it immediately, *(0.5) I thought thought of* it like a
Wendy:                                                                 *I never even thought of it*
Laura: (.) a couple *weeks ago.*
Wendy:                    *You already* thought of it?
     1.4
Laura: I thought- I thought, "Well, I actually have a lot of room, and I'm living alone. Should I do it?" And then I thought, "No,(0.5) I don't want to. I'd rather donate money."
     2.9
Wendy: I can understand that.

Notice how Wendy contributes to the redressive action by taking a one-down position ("I never even thought of it; you already thought of it?") and giving Laura the opportunity to show herself as generous. This is an example of collaborative social identity. Wendy helps Laura create her positive face of being generous and kind. The conflict is becoming resolved. Wendy first redresses Laura's negative face for offering the room without first consulting her, and then redresses her positive face by giving Laura a chance to show herself as generous. Laura, however, is not quite finished. She still attempts to find out what exactly Wendy had intended.

Laura: Actually, I just have to say something. I- I- I- just realized what made me feel bad. I know that you blurted it, and I know- I don't wanna hold you to it.(0.7) But it's like uh (3.8) there was a- th- jus- the feeling was like, somehow, like "Oh, you're paying for this room, so you could do whatever you want with it."
     2.0
Wendy:I don't feel *that way.*
Laura:         *But y-*      that's how- yeah, that's- yeah, it shocked me.
Like I- I- I felt like (0.9) shocked or something.(0.5) I know you don't feel that way, but that was somehow--
     1.3

Wendy:I'm sorry it came out *sounding* like that. I don't feel like that at all.
Laura:                                    *It's alright.*
Laura: It's OK.

Laura tries to equate the effect of Wendy's statement with Wendy's intent through prosodic cues: she "quotes" what she imagines Wendy to be saying. First, she sets off the intended utterance with the syntactic markers,

it's *like...*
the feeling was *like....*

*Like* is a marker used extensively to demarcate ensuing text. It is also often used to separate the text from the speaker, and thus minimize the force of an utterance and the speaker's responsibility for it. Literally, *like* denotes an approximation of something, not the thing itself. The speaker does not go on record with an exact statement, and therefore cannot be held responsible for the utterance. Here *like* is used as a syntactic marker that sets off the speaker (Laura) from her approximation of Wendy's intent. She attempts to interpret Wendy's utterance, and yet has to do so delicately. The attempt to identify the effect of a person's statements with his or her intent is an attempt to get that person to go on record. What would that bring? It has the advantage of providing a justification for a defense. The difficulty with indirect or off record utterances is that the recipient cannot directly defend or absolve him or herself, for there is no "proof" that the offending speech act has been committed.

Conflict situations show us how speakers' self-images implicitly assign, reject and perpetuate roles within relationships. Most of this happens off record, without raising the conflict to an explicit level. This preliminary research shows us that there could be several levels to the face threats in situations where conflict is explicit. In the situation above we found the speaker Laura to be in a *double bind* (Bateson, Jackson, Haley and Weakland, 1956): Wendy's speech act threatened Laura's positive and negative face. Her positive face needs constrained her from defending her negative face. She could not reject Wendy's imposition (defend her negative face wants) for fear of appearing selfish to others (protecting her positive face). We also witness an example of collaborative social identity. After face threatening Laura, Wendy takes a one-down position, and helps remedy her face threat by ratifying Laura's attempt to assert herself as a generous and altruistic person. Notice how every level of the conflict needs to be addressed: the face threat inherent in the content of Wendy's offer, the face threat inherent in Wendy offering something without consulting Laura, and the face threat inherent in Wendy's intent.

## 4. Rivalry

### 4.1. Rivalry versus conflict

Not every situation that we are analyzing as conflict would correspond to participants' perceptions. For instance, the participants in TR01 did not mention the presence of conflict, but spoke of "tension," "rivalry," "competition" and "aggression." Katz and Kahn differentiate competition from conflict in the following way:

> Like conflict, competition involves two or more systems, individual or social, engaged in activities that are in some sense incompatible; the successful completion of one precludes the successful completion of the other. By our definitions, however, competition itself involves no direct action of one party to interfere with the ongoing actions of the other. Should such interference and resistance occur, the competition would have become conflict (1966: 613-614).

Competitive or rivalrous interactions are marked by an absence of direct hindrance and resistance. Competition is a struggle with another individual for a role or self-image. Thus, we might say that our first example, the conflict between Wendy and Larry, is more competitive than conflictual. As we saw above, conflict need not be overt, and it is often the observer who attributes conflict to an interaction. Many of the interactions, particularly the one between Alain and Martin (TR01: "Let's make an agenda" -- "That's what we're doing") seem to be situations of rivalry rather than overt fights or conflict. Though we can define and differentiate conflict and competition, how can we differentiate them *in situ*? When is an interaction conflict and when is it competitive? Based on the empirical data, the following observations can be made.

Rivalry tended to occur more frequently and overtly where there is no *identified* (i.e., by name, assignment or rank) leader present. For instance, in TR01, the president was absent. The tone of that meeting was very different from TR04, where the president led the meeting. In addition, rivalry occurs where the social distance and/or power differences are minimal. That is, it occurs in relationships where power and/or social distance are close, e.g., between Laura and Wendy or between Alain and Martin, and George and Martin. Competition occurs most frequently between speakers of similar or close status, for only participants of similar status can contend for similar roles.

Rivalry tends not to occur between participants where the power difference is great. Rivalry implies a change in rank for the participant(s) initiating the rivalrous behavior. There is the implied hope or goal that through the challenge or rivalry an increase in rank and/or power will occur for the initiator. Thus, in situations where power is great, e.g. where leaders cannot be challenged, or where their fixed, institutional rank is great (such as a dictator, a person of higher caste, a teacher, a president, etc.) or because the people want to follow the leader (e.g., in the present community), rivalry will not occur between the identified leader and others. This is not to say that the leader's role cannot be disputed; it is frequently disputed, challenged, rejected, etc. The observation is that rivalry occurs in situations where individuals stand to gain rank and power by competing, and where there is minimal power and/or social distance. If a leader were to compete directly or overtly for power with a subordinate, it would be a sign that he or she was not in possession of power, and thus unsuited for the role.

## 4.2. Rivalry and performance

Rivalry is a feature in any group, not just this one. As we discussed above, the concept of face and self-image necessitates a degree of rivalry in that presenting one's own self-image automatically defines the self-image of the other. It is important to remember that presenting a particular self-image is an attempt to define oneself in a certain context, to a certain set of individuals. It needs to be ratified by others. For instance, in TR01, Alain suggests to Martin: "Let's make an agenda." Alain attempts to claim a role as executor or leader, the person getting things going. Yet this is what Martin has been doing throughout the meeting. Thus, Alain's statement and its implicit definition of himself defines Martin as *not* being the executor or leader.

The necessary conditions for this type of rivalry to occur is the presence of what Goffman termed "non-ratified overhearers," or, simply, audience members. An individual's social identity is created collaboratively, not just by speaker and listener, but by all the participants present. If, for example, Martin and Alain had had that same exchange in private, it would still have been seen as a competitive interaction. They may even have had an argument over it. In fact, even if Alain had gone on record and challenged Martin's leadership capabilities, it would still have remained a fight between the two men. Done in public, however, it becomes *a performance*. The other participants present become the ratifiers, amplifying the competitive atmosphere by siding with one man over the other to fulfill the leadership role. All those present in an interaction have the task of ratifying the others' social identities. It is the audience members whose responses and ratifications help create the social identities vied for. Therefore, presenting a self-image is an activity contingent upon audience members, those to whom one presents the self-image. The audience, as does any context, helps define the interaction. In the following section, we will see a situation of rivalry and performance in greater depth, when we analyze competition and cooperation.

## 4.3. Competition and cooperation

Rivalry is checked by cooperation in order to maintain the social relationships and community structure. Too much rivalry and competition between members endangers the community structures. As Bublitz says, conflict prevention and reduction is a primary social goal that insures the smooth functioning of human interaction. He maintains that social interaction should "be seen as the establishment and development of satisfactory social relationships between the fellow-speakers" (1988:140). Bublitz's conclusion, however, that speakers seek to establish and develop satisfactory relationships, misses the fact that if speakers are intent on *avoiding* and *reducing* conflict and tension, then this presupposes the presence of or potential for conflict and tension. In other words, conflict reduction is only necessary for situations which include or presuppose conflict and tension between speakers. Tension and conflict are present and in fact implicit in every interaction. Face-saving linguistic strategies presuppose face-threatening incidents. In fact, as we have discussed in Chapter 3, interactants strive to balance their tendency to assert their self-image with their need to preserve their group and their own standing within it. It seems interactions are characterized by both competition and cooperation, two aspects of one process of relational negotiation.

In our data, we have seen that there tend to be more rivalrous and competitive interactions between status equals or semi-equals than non-equals. Rivalry results from one participant presenting an image that defines, contradicts or constrains the self-image of the other. Rivalry is a competition for roles within a given set of social relationships, as we saw above with Alain and Martin. Furthermore, presenting a positive self-image necessitates someone to present it to. In the data, rivalrous situations are those where there are others present in addition to the two speakers. Thus, where there is an audience, roles are not only being contested among speakers, but are being *performed* as well. Performance is a necessary component of rivalry in that self-images need ratification by others. The presence of others can either help or hinder one's presentation of a self-image. For instance, in the Thanksgiving party where Wendy interrupts Larry's narrative (TR03), the audience ratifies the speakers' self-images. Wendy and Larry are competing to tell a story. Larry was in the midst of a narrative, and Wendy challenged his conclusions. Then she attempted to take the floor herself. Jean, a listener till then, asks a question. Wendy selects herself as the person to answer the question.

Jean: Well, why would he do that? I don't understand the psy*chology*.
Wendy:                                                  *So that* she likes
  him.(.) So that she doesn't give me a hard time.

Another situation of rivalry and performance is TR06, a dinner time chat in which Ellen is Laura's and Wendy's dinner guest. Ellen, the newcomer to the household and to the community, functions as an audience for Laura and Wendy, who use the opportunity to present their self-images. The dinner is the first time these three have been together in that particular grouping. Exchanging first impressions contributes to rivalry and performance. While self-images are created and performed in every interaction, in situations where the participants are first getting acquainted, more emphasis is placed on establishing and ratifying self-images.

...[A]n individual can more easily make a choice as to what line of treatment to demand from and extend to the others present at the beginning of an encounter than he can alter the line of treatment that is being pursued once the interaction is under way (Goffman, 1959:22).

During dinner, Laura and Wendy frequently intervene into each other's narratives. Ellen asks questions and shows interest in their narratives. Her questions, comments and responses ratify their images. Below, Ellen asks Laura why she is taping the conversation.

Laura: I'm taping it because I'm doing a study on uh (2.8) conversation, (0.5) and rules of discour- it's about rules of discourse. (0.9) uh (2.0) And it has to do with how people- (1.4) how people negotiate (1.5) the rules, (.) of conversation, and what that says about their relationships.
Ellen: Hmmm.
Laura: uh (0.7) like uh (1.2) things like (0.7) how people (0.7)
    [clears throat] take turns in conversation, how they establish who speaks next,
        *(0.7)* how do they- (1.4) how they negotiate
[Ellen: *aha*]
Laura: when (.) the floor's up for grabs, (0.5) and either one of you guys could speak.
    1.5
Laura: Like-
Wendy: Who's allowed to interrupt who.
Ellen: Mhmm.

Wendy makes a bid for co-narratorship. She attempts to develop the discourse topic with Laura, offering "Who's allowed to interrupt who" to the explanation. What do Laura's responses tell us? We see below that after an 0.8 second pause, Laura incorporates Wendy's contribution into her explanation.

Laura: Like all these-(.) there's all these like (.) ru::les,(.) that (.) you could see, once you transcribe it. It's like video analysis, in a w*ay*.
Ellen:                                          *It* sounds li*ke ???*.
Wendy:                                                    *You* should do it
    in a class, *like one* of your classes
Ellen:        *It's like--*
    1.3
Wendy: That happens so much, I notice, in classes.

Wendy offers a suggestion to Laura, and again tries to establish a collaborative floor. Wendy's attempt to co-develop the topic with Laura is rejected by Laura, we can surmise, in that she does not reply forthwith, but pauses for 1.3 seconds. This indicates that she considers this competitive rather than cooperative behavior. Not receiving an immediate response from Laura, Wendy continues, supplying the reason for her initial suggestion, and making a direct suggestion to Laura, going more on record in a bid for co-narratorship. Laura comes back onto the floor. Her self corrections perhaps indicate that her narrative as well as self-image as sole narrator and sole developer of the topic have been shaken.

> Laura: I do it (.) in- I do it (.) in the video class, when I talk about like uh (1.9) interventions and feedback. A lot of it's uh (0.9) through the conversation (.) between them.
> 0.5
> Ellen: Hmmm.

Laura's response to Wendy's question: "I do it, I do it," sounds like a defense, not an acceptance of Wendy's idea. The two seem to have different intentions. Wendy selects herself to co-develop the topic with Laura, yet Laura resists her attempt to share the floor. The text appears more easily understandable at the interactional rather than at the informational level. Laura's reply, "I do it, I do it," received no immediate response from Wendy. As we have seen, a lack of immediate response can point to ambivalence or lack of enthusiasm for a topic. Here, it indicates that Laura's response was not what Wendy had in mind.

> Laura: What did you have in mind though?
> 0.8
> Wendy: I meant (0.5) that you should tape the class.
> Laura: Oh. I should tape my cla *ss. I thought you* meant talk about it in class.
> Wendy:                                *Mhm yeah. An--*
> Wendy: No no.(1.0) No no. I meant (0.7) who interrupts who, like- (.) for example- like the class today. Like everyone's interrupting each other all the time.
> *(0.8)* Also my class-- I notice that.(1.2)
> Laura:   *Mhmm.*
> Wendy: I notice when I'm (2.3) taking a class, I'm like constantly interrupting

It seems as if Wendy intends to do more than bid for co-narrator of the discourse topic, but to raise her own discourse topic. Her initial suggestion ("You should do it in a class") was an opening attempt to discuss her own behavior in classes. From this interchange, we can see that rivalry or competition for the floor can be differentiated from collaboratively developed floors where two or more speakers develop a topic together. In a collaboratively developed floor, the responses build on each other; they create the topic together. As Edelsky (1981) says, collaboratively developed floors "provide high levels of communicative satisfaction...a sense of "we"-ness, excitement, fun, etc." In the present example, the contributions do not build or create a topic together, but each individual's contributions seem to take the other speaker away from her intended topic. Speakers' responses indicate that the others' contributions are a disruption from the intended train of thought or action. While a collaboratively developed floor is "we"-ness, rivalry is "I"-ness. Going back to the example, Laura finally manages to return to the topic of her work.

Laura:There was like a (.) unappropriate, (0.8) un (0.7) per-missible (0.5)
          *interruption.*
Wendy:  *I do that. Do* you remember? I d*i--*
Laura:                              *you* do that all the time.
   0.5
Wendy:Really?
   0.6
Laura: Yeah.
Wendy:I interrupt *so often.*
Laura:          *I mean ya-* I mean we all do it *all the time.*
Wendy:                              *Oh.*(1.0)

How does Laura negotiate Wendy's attempts to raise and develop her own topic? Laura's pauses and lack of listener response show a lack of interest in Wendy's contribution. She reduces the effectiveness of Wendy's contribution by minimizing it and her interest ("You do that all the time"), and later on, ("I mean we all do it all the time"). In other words, Laura refuses to be impressed. Her responses indicate that she is not willing to be an audience member to ratify Wendy's face. If a prerequisite for rivalry is an audience member to ratify one's self-image, then showing disinterest or remaining unimpressed is a strategy for denying the person the desired ratification of self-image. Thus, Laura manipulates this condition by not feeding the rivalry with the necessary listener responses.

Similar to the phenomenon of topic raising, many interactional acts require the ratification, approval or response of others for their successful completion. Rivalry which is not responded to or acknowledged does not succeed. Rivalry, like power, is a two-part act, a vehicle used to attain a particular self-image in front of, in contrast to, or beyond that of another.

In order for it to succeed, it needs ratification from the others present. There is thus an inherent insecurity in committing this act. Wendy continues her story obtaining ratification responses from Ellen, but not from Laura.

> Wendy: I specifically did it at-(1.5) at the *ausbildungs* committee. Martin was
> talking to someone, (0.8) and I- you remember?
> Ellen: I do remember. You interrupted, and he like kept talking, and finally like (.)
> --
> Wendy: and then he told me to wait. (0.8)
> Ellen: Mhmm, right.
> Wendy: I completely like- I didn't- (0.8) I didn't even notice.
>     2.3
> Laura: Well (.) the thing- the thing is, is like all these rules...

Laura fails to respond, and after a 2.3 seconds pause, she continues her narrative from before. She is clearly not ratifying Wendy's topic; in this case, she not only rejects the discourse topic, but the speech act itself. Her strategy for negotiating Wendy's rivalrous bid to raise a topic and share the floor is based on the precondition of ratification for rivalry. She refuses to "fan the fire" by contributing appropriate audience responses to the self-image Wendy is putting forward for ratification.


## 5. Summary

In sum, the preconditions for rivalry are that the contributing participants must have minimal social distance and have minimal difference in rank. Furthermore, the success of the self-image that one puts forward is dependent on the others' ratification. Rivalry is a performance of a given self-image which needs audience approval, e.g. appropriate responses, questions, replies, etc., which are addressed to the image that the person is putting forward. Withholding one's responses or replies is tantamount to denying the existence of the self-image, disagreeing with it or rejecting it. One reason not to ratify another's self-image is because it in some way challenges or negates that of the audience member refusing to participate. This is apparent in the following kinds of exchanges in which B negates A's statement, not for its information value, but for the implied self-image that the comment serves:

(TR01: Martin and Alain)
A: I have an idea. Let's make an agenda.
B: That's what we're doing.
(TR06: Wendy and Laura)
A: I interrupt so often.
B: I mean we all do it all the time.

As we have seen in Chapter 3, and again here, the factors of social distance and social status determine in part the type of interaction between interactants. It has been noted that conflict is addressed directly where social distance is at a minimum, while conflict remains encoded in the interaction itself when it occurs between members of different clusters. Rivalry is a type of conflict in which the ratification of self-image is at stake, and it occurs where social distance and/or power is at a minimum, i.e., between equals or semi-equals. We can see, therefore, from these examples that participants use many means within discourse to contest relationship roles such as rank and leadership. They use content and participation frameworks, contextual clues and even switching content in order to assign, reassign or avoid being assigned certain roles. As we saw with Michael and Huey, content may be used to develop a participation framework designed to switch the roles and hence ranks of participants.

To conclude, conflict arises where participants compete for certain positions of rank positions within the discourse. The social stratification that arises is not an objective, inherent quality of an individual but 1) depends on the ideology and values of the given society and 2) is a quality which, partly socially determined, is nonetheless contested through various strategies of discourse.

# Chapter Six: Power and Status in the Community

## 1. Introduction

Verbal interaction, as we have seen throughout this study, is constrained by the social relationships between the interactants: their status, their proximity or distance, amount of contact, by the demands of a particular social situation, and finally, by the norms and values of the particular speech community. Constraints, in the sense that I am using the term, are limitations on behavior, and make up the implicit or unconscious rules which ensure that discourse is orderly, coherent and successful. They are the framework for the interaction, so to speak, providing a structure within and through which speakers construct meanings. As Goffman points out, behavior is accorded meaning whether or not it follows rules of conduct:

> An act that is subject to a rule of conduct is, then, a communication. ...An act that is subject to rules of conduct but does not conform to them is also a communication - often even more so - for infractions make news and often in such a way as to disconfirm the selves of the participants. Thus rules of conduct transform both action and inaction into expression, and whether the individual abides by the rules or breaks them, something significant is likely to be communicated (1967:51).

Constraints on behavior, whether they take the form of hierarchical caste or status systems, group norms and ideologies, or the demands of social distance or proximity, transform action into expression. Behavior, including verbal behavior, is meaningful only against a backdrop of a standard, or a rule. We imbue behavior with meaning in so far as it conforms to our expectations, to the societal norms and to the moral constraints placed upon it.

Speech is behavior whose meaning is a function of the expectations of a certain context, the constraints between speakers, and the constraints internal to language itself. For instance, we saw in Chapters 3 and 4 how the violation of a linguistic rule of coherence (Grice's (1975) Maxim of Quantity) created meaning: Ulrike asked Laura to provide information about the seminar day leaders. Rather than continuing on the expected train of thought ("Peter's doing the first day, and...") Laura diverged from the expectations ("and teachers are expected to do what they want..."), thereby investing her behavior with meaning: she was uninformative, vague, and unwilling or unable to fulfill her role as resource person.

The ability to adhere to, violate or manipulate norms and constraints is communicative competence (cf. Gumperz, 1982). When a speaker uses communicative competence to influence others' behavior, to achieve a position as a resource person or to increase his or her status, we speak of political effectiveness. Speakers in this community achieve political effectiveness through manipulating and exploiting norms and expectations and choosing among items in a repertoire, thereby signaling social meaning. The speaker who can exploit expectations about the dialect and standard features of a code, for instance, does not just choose variables, but, by choosing items from a particular repertoire, exploits participants' knowledge of the variables, of the shared norms and values, and of the situation, and demonstrates his or her control over a range of choices. By exploiting variables internal to a group or network the speaker "exploits symbols of identity to achieve communicative ends" (Gumperz, 1989). Symbols of identity are these norms and constraints, and a member's political influence in the community is demonstrated by his or her ability, not only to exploit, but also to create symbols of membership and ideology.

In sum, the social constraints of a network, shared values, expectations or social relationships provide the structure within which speakers choose variables to construct meanings. In Chapter 1, I defined power as a self-image which requires ratification from the other participants. It is not a commodity which can be taken by force, but, as a role which requires ratification, needs to be negotiated throughout the interaction. The data reveal that individuals exercise power in their ability to create, exploit and operate effectively within group norms to (momentarily) influence others.

This chapter is divided as follows. First, the social structure and interactional style of the community will be discussed on the basis of the findings from the data. Specifically, we shall look at politic verbal behavior, rhetorical political strategies and conflict and competition in discourse. We will then discuss how the data show power to be a consensual process and the implications this has for sociology and studies of discourse. Finally, the method of analyzing interaction as speakers' topics and topical actions will be evaluated, and its strengths and weaknesses discussed. I will discuss the extent to which this method provided greater insights into speakers' verbal behavior. In addition, the study combined network methods with discourse analysis in order to situate the interactions in context, to provide information about the social relationships between the speakers, and to explain problems of communication between speakers. I will also discuss the limitations of this method and the extent to which it succeeded in illuminating problems of verbal interaction, status and power in communities of the mind. Finally, points of further research will be mentioned. What are our next steps? Has an ethnographic analysis helped to extend the analysis of discourse in groups? What are its limitations? Can this method of analysis be applied to other groups?

## 2. Interaction and social identity

This study has attempted to show a different view of social identity and discourse. The sociolinguistic view has typically seen talk as constrained by the social features of context and by the social identities of the participants. In this study, however, we are equally concerned with the way in which participants' talk determines, creates and shapes their and others' social identities. This work has set out to show how discourse is a primary social activity which contributes to assigning, shaping and reshaping social identities. Interactants contest and compete for roles and self images through discourse, and, in so doing, collaboratively create their own and ratify each other's social identities and self-images.

### 2.1. Politic behavior

This continual process of creating social identities necessitates that verbal interaction is laden with potential conflict. Every interaction is a minefield of potential social gaffes, confrontations, insults, offenses and humiliations. When we attempt to present a particular self-image, we run the risk of offending others by competing with them for the same role. We run the risk of offending others by implicitly assigning them an inferior role when we take on a role ourselves. And we also run the risk of humiliating ourselves if our attempts to take on a particular role are ignored or rejected by others. This description of verbal interaction is similar to, yet broader and more encompassing than that suggested by Brown and Levinson (1978, 1987). Their theory of polite verbal behavior is useful for considering language as act-by-act sequences, in which one act causes a face threat which must then be redressed or repaired. Rather than view FTAs in sequential, causal relationships, and polite verbal behavior as an utterance or linguistic gambit which repairs or redresses face threats, we take Watts' (1989) view of discourse as politic verbal behavior. We need to see the entire interaction as politic verbal behavior, where participants negotiate their need to promote positive self-image and promote their power and status vis-a-vis the other, while avoiding serious threats to the interaction lest their own standing in the community be jeopardized.

We noted that speakers used various strategies to satisfy this dual demand. The strategies they employ depend on the severity of imposition of the face threat, their social distance to other interactants, their status vis-a-vis other participants, and also on the speech situation. Speakers shift their participation framework, that is, the relationship between themselves and what is being said in order to invoke different relationship identities between participants. For instance, speakers would use statements of personal preference, feelings and needs in situations where it would seem inappropriate. However, this strategy served to intensify one's topic and in some cases to protect the topic from being rejected. Speakers had more difficulty going on record rejecting someone else's topic if the speaker identified personally with his or her topic.

## 2.2. Rhetorical strategies

Speakers not only use polite linguistic strategies, but they exploit their knowledge of the norms of the community and norms of politic verbal behavior in order to create meanings. For instance, knowing that close social distance and intimacy is often conveyed through solidarity politeness and, in some cases, direct confrontation and bald face threatening acts, speakers would sometimes use solidarity politeness strategies in order to achieve political effectiveness. In formal speech situations with greater social distance between participants, it was found that some of the higher ranking members of the community, while more distant socially, actually achieved political effectiveness by using solidarity politeness and thus sounding more collegial. They would present topics as personal preferences or desires, use pronouns of solidarity ("we", "let's", "what do you think?"), use personal narrative or story telling to illustrate ideas, and, in one instance, explicitly request permission to take the floor in a situation where turns were locally managed. Political effectiveness works in both directions. It was found that both high status and lower status individuals used strategies which oriented their speaking styles towards a target group. Lower status members tended to use deference and formality strategies when speaking to emphasize their authority, and achieve political effectiveness.

### 2.3. Topic analysis and power

By revising the economic model of turn-taking in our analysis and using a topic analysis, we have brought to light interactional strategies speakers use beyond those for getting and maintaining the floor. Speakers contest their rank and exert power through topical actions: bringing in ideas, rejecting others' ideas, being listened to and agreed with by others when saying something, having others follow a suggestion or advice, etc. Speakers relate to their topics. They identify with what it is they want to say, not necessarily with the length or quantity of their turns. When speakers raise a topic, they are attempting to take the position of resource person, a position of temporary leadership. They are also, however, placing themselves in a vulnerable position. Their positive self-image depends upon the acknowledgment and support of others.

Since topics consist of speech acts (the intent to say something) and discourse topics (what the speaker has to say), raising a topic thus needs dual ratification; the speech act needs to be ratified, and the idea or discourse topic needs to be accepted in order to avoid a potentially face threatening situation. If a speaker's topic is not ratified, if it is met with silence, speakers will prompt others for a response, reformulate, reiterate or supply synonyms for the idea in the hope that others will accept it. In the case that no support or recognition is forthcoming, speakers will be forced to abandon their own topic. In the case that the speech act is ratified, that is, a speaker raises a topic and the subject is under discussion, if the idea meets with resistance or strong disinterest, the speaker may be obliged to withdraw the topic from the floor in order to avoid impinging upon the other speakers' negative face. This is especially true in small task groups. The speaker who raises a topic which is being rejected, debated, or only very minimally discussed, can be said to be committing a face threat by not withdrawing it. He or she is threatening the negative face wants of the other participants by forcing them to go on record rejecting the idea. In the interest of the entire interaction, speakers thus withdraw their own topic or stalemate a meeting indefinitely.

## 2.4. Conflict and competition

Social constraints against conflict in public curtail the amount of conflict one observes among adults in free verbal interaction. There are, however, countless examples of competition, rivalry and covert conflict in discourse. In fact, as we have noted earlier, all verbal interactions may be considered competitive, potentially conflictual situations. Social distance and social status determine in part the type of interaction between interactants. Where social distance is at a minimum, there is a greater chance that conflict will be addressed directly. Direct confrontation between speakers of minimal social distance can even be seen as a solidarity marker. Covert conflict, where it remains embedded in the interaction itself, occurs more often between members of greater social distance and different statuses.

Participants will be more likely to admit to competition than to conflict in an interaction. Rivalry and competition can be differentiated from conflict as a type of conflict in which the ratification of one's self-image or the attainment of a certain position opposes the wishes of another. It occurs where social distance and/or power is at a minimum, i.e., between equals or semi-equals. For participants to engage in competitive behavior, both must stand to gain something from the rivalry. Thus, we rarely see mutual competition between a member of high status and a member of lower status.

Another important characteristic of rivalry and competition is that the success of the self-image that one puts forward depends on the others' ratification. Thus, competition is a type of verbal interaction requiring the presence of an audience; speakers are contesting a role by performing a given self-image, and soliciting the appropriate responses to that self-image from the audience. In other words, presenting a self-image is a two-part act. The first part is the presentation, but the second part, just as important, if not more, is the ratification and acknowledgment of that image. Withholding one's responses or ratification is a way of refuting, denying or rejecting one's self-image. This need for ratification means that self-images and social identities are constructed collaboratively out of the presentation of the self, on the one hand, and out of the others' ratification and acknowledgment, on the other hand. Thus, the conflict and competition in discourse results from the process of speakers shaping and reshaping their social identities.

## 3. Implications for power

We have seen in the data that the traditional concept of power, e.g., as Polsby (1963) defines it, is insufficiently complex to explain the strategies and methods of political influence in verbal interaction. Polsby's definition of power is

> the capacity of one actor to do something affecting another actor which changes the probable pattern of specified future events. This can be envisaged most easily in a decision-making situation (1963:3-4).

It falls short on a number of different points. The present study provides a concept of power which is less causally and more dynamically oriented. Power, as actors in verbal interaction display it, is not so much a possession, as a capacity or strategy available to all members in an interaction, regardless of local or institutional rank. It shows up in members' abilities to negotiate the images and roles that are assigned in an interaction, through the statements and utterances of others. Even the participant said to possess lower rank has options, strategies and devices at his or her disposal to contest, dispute and challenge the roles assigned to him or her by others. These strategies might be embedded and implicit in an utterance, carried by unintended levels of communication, and hence deniable. Actors' rank perhaps do not permit them to challenge or exercise power overtly, yet they are forced to do so anyway, as we saw in TR01, where Laura and the organizers did not have the authority to provide certain information. Instead, they went off record to do so.

Another problem with Polsby's definition of power is that it limits its occurrence to situations where one person affects the behavior of another, hence, to situations where an actor is trying to get something from another actor, i.e., decision-making situations, conflicts and competitions. Yet as the data show, all social interaction is the continual assignment and negotiation of self-images and their ensuing roles. In every verbal interaction we may witness participants negotiating roles, images and status; we need not wait for overt conflict to witness the use of rhetorical strategies to achieve political effectiveness. As with politic behavior, a repair does not follow a face threat; the imposition or challenge comes hand in glove with a device to "soften" or minimize it.

A further problem with the definition is that it presupposes unity of will or intention. Ulterior motives, secondary gain, or opposing, conflicting or dual intentions are not considered. This stands in contrast to the concept of politic behavior as we have been using it. The theory upon which the politeness model is based posits a dual intention. The actor is constrained by a need to assert self-image, to impose, to achieve status over other participants. At the same time the actor needs to minimize the imposition in order to preserve the social relationships. If people only had single intentions, politeness in language would be nonexistent. As Lukes says, the proponents of the foregoing view of power

> are opposed to any suggestion that interests might be unarticulated or unobservable, and above all, to the idea that people might actually be mistaken about, or unaware of, their own interests (1974:14).

Polsby's definition also falls short in excluding intuitive and lay concepts of power which actors might be using in their interactions. Lukes (1974) points out that the traditional concept of power is "power over" someone or something. Yet when lay persons speak of power, they not only speak of "power over" an individual or group, but frequently "power to" do something. The lay concept of "power to" is closer to our view of it as the ability to negotiate roles. One cannot "force" another to take on a role.

The former idea of power refers to individuals or groups who have an effect on others, or who, by decree or institutional investiture, make certain claims and effect the behavior of others. The latter idea refers to the ability or capacity to negotiate roles in discourse and to take on the role of momentary resource person. One of the difficulties with sociological and linguistic studies which deal with the "problem of power" in the helping professions is that the two concepts are frequently equated. What researchers fail to take into account is the concept of power as a characteristic of a given situation, speaker or group. For instance, Davis (1988) in a study of power in the discourse of medical interviews, analyzes power between doctors and patients. Yet she assumes that the occurrences of power and power abuse will automatically arise from the (male) doctors, i.e., that their institutional rank (and gender) invests them with power.

The view we have been putting forward, however, is that power is effective verbal rhetoric which rallies the consent of the others. Effective strategies are those that are followed by the others. The data have shown that the effective arguments are clothed in the repertoire of the target individual or group; the powerful member assumes the wants and the needs of the other in order to achieve his or her goals. In fact, truly effective rhetoric is not easy to identify. By definition, it is not overt, but covert. Power which changes minds, which "mobilizes bias," and which persuades others to follow is not exercised through a blatant show of force, or even through open conflict. It is, rather, a subtle and sophisticated strategy which can change minds.

## 3.1. Power as consensual

The type of rhetorical strategy used by the higher ranking members in this community reveals that leadership and power are not exercised by force or formal decree. The hierarchical structures of the community are in part created by the institutional rank of the members, but they have to be perpetuated and maintained through political action. That is, one cannot rely on institutional rank alone as a marker of power. The individual must work for his or her power and position, and maintaining and perpetuating it is contingent upon the approval and consent of the membership at large. Thus, the traditional notion of power whereby an individual gets something from or does something to others against their will cannot explain the interactions between speakers from the present data. Rather, political power is seen here as dependent upon the

continued ratification and consensus of the people, both of which are
obtained most effectively through strategies of politic behavior.

Specifically, speakers use solidarity-claiming strategies, whereby they
adapt the others' wants as their own. This is, however, more than a mere
manipulation of group norms. Its effectiveness lies in the fact that it
serves a group need as well; it creates and strengthens group identity and
structure. This works in part because groups need structure, purpose and
identity, and because the individual needs to belong and be integrated
into a larger group. The effective leader serves the group by supporting
and perpetuating its identity and spirit. In fact, the need for individuals to
belong to a group with a solid identity leaves them open to leaders with
nefarious and dubious intents.

In any case, the interactions in this community reveal that leadership is
something that is continually contested between individuals, as seen in
the rivalrous nature of encounters. Self-images need to be continually
ratified and renewed in every encounter. Thus leaders and higher status
individuals, and those bidding for increased rank or power are in
vulnerable positions. If power is consensual, then the powerful individual
is insecure, for his or her role must be ratified and renewed by the others.
Here again, we see that equating individuals with one role, strategy or
theme alone fails. The idea of power as a consensual, continually
negotiable capacity means that no one individual in an interaction is
"powerful" or "weak." One can possess institutional rank or authority, but
power or political effectiveness can be achieved by any speaker. The one
who raises topics, bids for power or presents a self-image depends on
audience ratification, and is thus in an insecure or even weak position at
certain moments. Furthermore, the one who is requested to confirm or
ratify another speaker's self-image has the power to deny or reject a bid
by anyone else. As we saw between Laura and Wendy, for instance,
Wendy interrupted and competed with Laura for the turn at talk.
Traditionally, we might see Wendy as exercising power over Laura. Yet
Laura had various strategies at her disposal to counteract Wendy's bid.
She chose to withhold attending to Wendy's narrative, thus placing
Wendy in a "weaker" role, for the moment.

Consensual power means that social identities are constructed
collaboratively with our fellow interactants, competitors and opponents.
The role that another takes for herself or himself will directly affect the

roles that we may take for ourselves. Identity is a collective process. It is created out of the roles which we choose for ourselves, the roles that others are claiming for themselves, and out of the audience's approval or disapproval for these roles.

## 4. Methodological considerations

I have attempted to analyze relationships in a social network, in particular the exercise of power and status, through verbal interaction. The method of analysis challenged the strictly economic approach to conversational structure by seeing that speakers compete for the role of resource person by controlling the topic, an activity which subsumes numerous interactive and verbal strategies. The analysis of topics and topical actions has challenged the idea that the participant who talks the most, or the longest, has the most power. As topics and speakers need to be ratified, taking a turn at talk is not always identical with power. Further, because topics need to be ratified, accepted and developed throughout the course of an interaction, we need an analysis that covers the entire exchange, otherwise we would be led to the false conclusion that one exercises or gains power by speaking. The negotiation for power following the introduction of a new topic is not apparent to the observer who merely sees a dyadic exchange. The analysis of a strip of talk must include how it is received by others, as well as the participation framework invoked by the utterance, a structure that encompasses, among other phenomena, the addressee of the talk as well as its speaker (Goodwin and Goodwin, 1990:109).

The method of topical analysis has been particularly useful in combination with a network analysis, for we are able to see more than a two-dimensional view of interaction; we can see who the speakers are, their relationships to each other and how they negotiate these relationships through interaction. Because topical analysis considers talk over time, we have more access to the full range of speakers' strategies. We therefore witness the insecurity of the "powerful" speaker, and hence, see a consensual aspect to power.

The analysis is a qualitative study; we have not isolated individual variables which could be tested in other situations. Our findings are in keeping with the ethnographic paradigm it employs. This study attempted to describe a particular community and to find the patterns of interaction in the social context. Due to the type of community under investigation, certain social variables, such as socio-economic class, were not useful in revealing the patterns of interaction. Instead, the social variables that are internally meaningful to the community were brought out using a network analysis.

The initial network breakdown of the relationships and statuses between members provides an insight into situations of rivalry, leadership and conflict. For instance, rivalry, conflict and the extent to which speakers went off record could be directly related to network features. Rivalry was most prevalent between speakers of similar status. The greater the status difference, the less the occurrence of rivalry. Conflict, on the other hand, which was overt, i.e., referred to explicitly, only occurred between speakers of close social proximity. Finally, the greater the social contact between speakers, the likelier they were to go on record, to use fewer linguistic strategies of politeness, and to challenge each others' topics and turns. Cross cluster interaction, or interaction between speakers of greater social distance, was marked by deference strategies of politeness: speakers went off record, were conventionally indirect, and redressed their potential FTAs.

Many of the verbal interactions in the data would not have been meaningful to the observer without a network analysis and a breakdown of the significant social variables, features and norms of the community. Thus, though it is not always possible to study verbal interaction within its social environment, I believe that, as far as possible, the entire backdrop of culture needs to be brought into its analysis. Although isolating significant variables and correlating them quantitatively is a useful and important endeavor, it fails to account for different repertoires and strategies not adhering to strict classifications. For instance, in this study, effective strategies could not be associated only with the particular members, but were found among all speakers.

It also appears that problems of interaction and communication are problems of network membership and group values as well. The two are inextricably tied. Rivalry and conflict in interaction can be understood as speakers' attempts to reassign cluster membership, to increase rank or to bridge social distance. When a member attempts to increase his or her rank, or to shift his or her position in the network, this has a "ripple" effect, leading to continual adjustments in the entire network. For instance, presenting a self-image, as we have seen, necessarily defines or re-defines the communication partner. In TR03, the Thanksgiving party, Wendy's challenge of Larry's narrative, and his interpretation of the event, re-defined her role in the moment as therapist rather than party guest, and thus automatically reassigned his role as well to that of client.

## 4.1. Implications for further study

In attempting to reconstruct social relationships on the basis of recorded interactions in natural settings, this study was able to uncover a number of important theoretical and practical points for further research. To begin with, we must ask ourselves to what extent the ethnography of one particular community of the mind can provide us with information about other types of communities, and about the special problems of sub-cultures and political organizations.

From a methodological perspective, there seems to be only minimal differences between communities held together by regional or geographical features, and communities held together by shared interests and values. The decisive factor appears to be the individuals' own identification with a particular community. As I mentioned in Chapter 1, the borders between these two types of communities are fuzzy, and there is a fair amount of overlap. In fact, this type of analysis could be just as easily carried out in a geographical community. The study has shown that membership hinges upon identifying the significant social variables and the particular norms of the community, factors which are equally observable in both types of communities.

Second, though we were, for the most part, successful in our goal of reconstructing the social structures based on the recorded data, the limited scope of the study necessarily excluded many issues, interactions and features of the community. For instance, the bi-dialectal nature of the community played only a minor role in the study, yet has the potential to provide us with a wealth of information about languages in contact, codes and repertoires and code-switching mechanisms in a network. In fact, the amount of analyzed recorded material was daunting, and a small amount of data yielded a surprising amount of material. Only 11 hours were transcribed from a total of 17 hours of recorded interactions. Of those 11 hours, only a few minutes ended up in these pages.

A number of related studies could be undertaken. In particular, it would be worthwhile to study the continued growth and change of the community. Follow-up studies could investigate shifts in the network structure, social relationships and changes in interactional style. Furthermore, other political or task oriented groups could be investigated to see if there are similarities in interaction. Finally, ethnographic analyses of different types of communities of the mind, political, task oriented, business, academic and ethnic groups etc. could be compared to discover patterns of social interaction in context, the nature of cooperation and competition, and problems of ideology and membership.

Further study could also be conducted on communities, membership and ideology in a variety of situations, particularly with other political organizations. The data concentrated upon verbal interaction between speakers in a social network; we were not able to obtain much information about communities, membership and ideology, or the rise and fall of political organizations and policy. I envisage a further study of an organization which is in the process of disbanding, or a long term study of a political organization over time, as it grows, shifts and changes.

Of particular importance in this study were the theoretical conclusions we were able to draw about power, particularly the view that power can be a negotiable, interactive variable which all participants have access to. This finding surely needs to be tested in a variety of situations and contexts, including situations which are more explicitly hierarchical. In fact, a possible further step would be to study instances where institutional rank is explicitly tied to power, such as doctor-patient relations, teacher-student, family relations, etc. to test the hypothesis that power is consensual and negotiated, and that roles are collaboratively constructed.

The task that this study set out to accomplish, that of reconstructing social relationships through interaction, has raised other unexpected, theoretical points. In particular, it has led me to consider problems of meaning and communication, both intended and unintended. While the observer is able to listen to speakers' interactions after the fact, what the speakers understand, intend and communicate in real time still remains a mystery of verbal interaction. Whether or not the insights that the observer obtains can ever be tested by speakers' perceptions in real time interaction remains to be seen. In fact, once we establish that the meaning of an utterance need not be limited to an outer referent, we are left with the sticky problem of having to determine what an utterance means. The task of establishing how social meanings are constructed, whether speakers intend to communicate them and ways for listeners to interpret them is a difficult one indeed.

While this study has isolated a few methods and strategies for speakers to convey social meanings, particularly their relationships to interlocutors, much work remains to be done in the field. In particular, there needs to be a comprehensive theory of how speakers construct and communicate meanings in interaction. Until such a theory is constructed, we can only be satisfied with partial analyses and tentative conclusions.

The study of interaction in communities is a timely one; it has widespread implications in the modern world as people migrate and move, join cultures and groups, disband and move on. We spend most of our lives in groups of some kind: at school, at the workplace, in the neighborhood, in the family, etc. In fact, we belong to many groups at once, and, without even being aware of it, we develop the cultural fluency necessary to be a member in many different groups simultaneously. The way an individual develops the fluency to be a functioning, effective member of a group appears to be an automatic procedure, happening again and again, whenever people merge and join. In fact, it seems we only become aware of our cultural fluency when we fail to attain it, or when an individual steps outside the boundaries of membership to challenge the existing norms.

# Appendix

**Part I.**

a. Name up to 5 people whom you would go to for advice or consultation if you were having
   serious difficulties with a case or in a teaching situation.

b. Imagine a meeting in which there was a good deal of arguing and little being accomplished.
   After awhile, someone has an idea for a solution that most everyone present agrees to.
   Name up to 5 people whom you think likely to be the one with the solution.

c. If the institute had to elect one president for a year, name up to 5 people under whose
   leadership you would feel secure.

d. Name up to five people whom you most frequently see socially.

**Part II.**

a. What is your nationality?

b. What is your mother tongue?

c. Are you male or female?

d. Which of the following groups do you belong to?

- group practice
- student body
- diploma candidate
- diplomates
- original Swiss "Grandparents""
- teaching staff at the Intensive Courses. If so, since when and in what capacity (teacher,
  assistant)

e. Do you belong to any committees such as executive committee, training committee,
   Intensive Course planning committee, etc.?

f. Do you donate your time and service to the organization for free or for minimal pay, such
   as revising brochures, budget, newsletter, etc.?

g. Do you give seminars (more than one day) in Switzerland?

h. Do you give seminars (more than one day) outside Switzerland? If so, where and
   approximately how many a year?

i. What is your current level of education?

j. Do you have or are you working on an advanced degree? If so, which and at what
   institution or university?

k. How long have you been affiliated with the institute? If your affiliation precedes the institute's founding, how long have you been associated with Peter?

l. For North Americans, How long have you been living in Zurich?


**Part III.**

(For North Americans) Can you speak High German? (HG) Can you speak Swiss German? (SG) Do you use HG or SG in your work? How often: (always, usually, sometimes, occasionally, seldom, never)

(For Swiss) Can you speak English? Do you use English in your work? If so, how often: (always, usually, sometimes, occasionally, seldom, never)

# Bibliography

Austin, J.L.
    1962.    *How to Do Things with Words.* Oxford: Clarendon Press.

Bachrach, P. and Baratz, M.
    1970.    *Power and Poverty. Theory and Practice.* New York: Oxford University Press.

Bales, R.F.
    1950.    *Interaction Process Analysis.* Chicago: The University of Chicago Press.

Bales, R.F.
    1970.    *Personality and Interpersonal Behavior.* New York: Holt, Rinehart and Winston.

Bales, R.F.
    1973.    "Communication in Small Groups." In George Miller (ed.), *Communication, Language, and Meaning.* New York: Basic Books, 208-218.

Barnes, J.A.
    1954.    "Class and Committee in a Norwegian Island Parish." *Human Relations*, 8. 39-58.

Barnes, J.A.
    1969.    "Networks and Political Processes." In J.C. Mitchell (ed.), *Social Networks in Urban Situations.* Manchester: Manchester University Press, 51-76.

Bateson, G.
    1951.    "Information and Codification: a Philosophical Approach." In Juergen Ruesch and Gregory Bateson (eds.), *Communication: The Social Matrix of Psychiatry.* New York: Norton, 168-211.

    1972.    *Steps to an Ecology of Mind.* New York: Ballantine.

Bateson, G., Jackson, D.D., Haley, J. and Weakland, J.
    1956.    "Towards a Theory of Schizophrenia." *Behavioral Science*, 1:4. 251-64.

Bavelas, J., Rogers, L.E. and Millar, F.E.
    1985.    "Interpersonal Conflict." In T. van Dijk (ed.), *Handbook of Discourse Analysis, Vol. 4: Discourse Analysis in Society.* London: Academic Press. 9-26.

Bennett, A.
   1981.   "Interruptions and the Interpretation of Conversation". *Discourse Processes*, 4. 171-188.
Bereiter, C., Engelman, S., Osborn, J. and Reidford, P.A.
   1966.   "An Academically Oriented Pre-school Program for Culturally Deprived Children. " In F.M. Hechinger (ed.), *Pre-school Education Today*. New York: Doubleday.
Berger, P.L.
   1963.   *Invitation to Sociology*. Garden City, New York: Anchor Books.
Berger, P.L. and Luckmann, T.
   1966.   *The Social Construction of Reality*. New York: Doubleday & Co. (Anchor Books, 1967).
Bernstein, B.
   1971.   *Class, Codes and Control*. London: Routledge and Kegan Paul.
   1972.   "A Sociolinguistic Approach to Socialization; With Some Reference to Educability." In John Gumperz and Dell Hymes (eds.), *Directions in Sociolinguistics*. Oxford: Basil Blackwell. 465-497.
Blom, J.P. and Gumperz, J. J.
   1972.   "Social Meaning in Linguistic Structures." In John Gumperz and Dell Hymes (eds.), *Directions in Sociolinguistics*. Oxford: Basil Blackwell. 407-434.
Bloomer, D.
   1965.   "Hesitation and Grammatical Encoding." *Language and Speech*, 8. 148-158.
Boas, F.
   1911.   *Introduction to Handbook of American Indian Languages* (Smithsonian Institution, Bureau of American Etnnology, Bulletin 40). Washington, D.C.: U.S. Government Printing Office. 1-83.
Boissevain, J.
   1974.   *Friends of Friends: Networks, Manipulators and Coalitions*. Oxford: Blackwell.
Bott, E.
   1957.   *Family and Social Network*. London: Tavistock Press.
Boulding, K.
   1962.   *Conflict and Defense*. New York: Harper and Row.
Brown, G. and Yule, G.
   1983.   *Discourse Analysis*. Cambridge: Cambridge University Press.

Brown, P. and Levinson, S.
   1978.    "Universals in Language Usage: Politeness Phenomena. " In E. Goody
            (ed.), *Questions and Politeness: Strategies in Social Interaction*. London:
            Cambridge University Press. 56-289.
   1979.    "Social Structure, Groups and Interaction. " In K. Scherer and H. Giles
            (eds.), *Social Markers in Speech.* Cambridge: Cambridge University
            Press. 291-341.
   1987.    *Politeness: Some Universals in Language Usage.* Cambridge:
            Cambridge University Press.
Brown, P. and Fraser, C.
   1979.    "Speech as a Marker of Situation. " In K. Scherer and H. Giles (eds.),
            *Social Markers in Speech.* Cambridge: Cambridge University
            Press.33-62.
Brown, R.
   1986.    *Social Psychology.* The Second Edition. New York: The Free Press.
Bublitz, W.
   1988.    *Supportive Fellow-Speakers and Cooperative Conversations.* Amsterdam
            and Philadelphia: John Benjamins Publishing Company.
Butterworth, B., Hine, R.R. and Brady, K.D.
   1977.    "Speech and Interaction in Sound-only Communication Channels."
            *Semiotica*, 20: 1/2. 81-99.
Chafe, W.
   1979.    "The Flow of Thought and the Flow of Language. " In T. Givon (ed.),
            *Syntax and Semantics, vol. 12. Discourse and Syntax.* New York:
            Academic Press. 159-182.
Cheshire, J.
   1982.    *Variation in an English Dialect: A Sociolinguistic Study.* Cambridge:
            Cambridge University Press.
Cole, P. and Morgan, J. (eds.).
   1975.    *Syntax and Semantics 3: Speech Acts.* New York: Academic Press.
Crystal, D.
   1975.    *The English Tone of Voice.* New York: St. Martin's Press.
Dahl, R.A.
   1957.    "The Concept of Power." *Behavioral Science*, 2.201-5.
Davis, K.
   1988.    *Power Under the Microscope.* Dordrecht: Foris Publications.

Dittmann, A.T. and L.G. Llewellyn.
   1968.   "Relationship between Vocalisations and Head Nods as Listener Responses." *Journal of Personality and Social Psychology*, 9. 79-84.
Duncan, S.
   1972.   "Some Signals and Rules for Taking Speaking Turns in Conversations." *Journal of Personality and Social Psychology*, 23:2. 283-292.
   1973.   "Toward a Grammar for Dyadic Conversation." *Semiotica*, 9. 29-46.
   1975.   "On the Structure of Speaker-auditor Interaction During Speaking Turns." *Language in Society*, 2. 161-180.
Duncan, S. and Fiske, D.
   1977.   *Face-to-face Interaction: Research, Methods, and Theory*. Hillsdale, N.J.: Lawrence Erlbaum Associates.
   1985.   *Interaction Structure and Strategy*. Cambridge: Cambridge University Press.
Duncan, S. and Niederehe, G.
   1974.   "On Signalling That It's Your Turn to Speak." *Journal of Experimental Social Psychology*, 10. 234-247.
Durkheim, E.
   1953.   *Sociology and Philosophy*. Transl. D.F. Pocock. Glencoe, Ill.: Free Press.
Edelsky, C.
   1981.   "Who's Got the Floor?" *Language in Society*, 10. 383-421.
Ferguson, C.A.
   1959.   "Diglossia." *Word*, 15. 325-40.
Ferguson, N.
   1977.   "Simultaneous Speech, Interruptions and Dominance." *British Journal of Social Clinical Psychology*, 16. 295-302.
Foucault, M.
   1980.   *Power/Knowledge: Selected interviews and other writings 1972-1977*. Great Britain: The Harvester Press.
French, P. and Local, J.
   1986.   "Prosodic Features and the Management of Interruptions." In Catherine Johns-Lewis (ed.), *Intonation in Discourse*. London and Sydney: Croom Helm. 157-180.
Geertz, C.
   1973.   *The Interpretation of Culture*. New York: Basic.
Gerth, H.H. and Mills, C.W.
   1953.   *Character and Social Structure*. New York: Harcourt, Brace and Co.

Goffman, E.
  1959.    *The Presentation of Self in Everyday Life*. Harmondsworth, Middlesex:
           Penguin Books.
  1967.    *Interaction Ritual*. New York: Pantheon Books.
  1981.    *Forms of Talk*. Oxford: Basil Blackwell.
Goldman-Eisler, F.
  1958.    "Speech Analysis and Mental Processes." *Language and Speech*, 1.
           59-75.
Good, C.
  1979.    "Language as a Social Activity: Negotiating Conversation." *Journal of
           Pragmatics*, 3. 151-167.
Goodwin, C. and Goodwin, M.
  1990.    "Interstitial argument." In Alan Grimshaw (ed.), *Conflict Talk*.
           Cambridge: Cambridge University Press. 85-117.
Goodwin, M.H.
  1980     "Directive/response Speech Sequences in Girls' and Boys' Task
           Activities." In McConnell-Ginet, R. Borker,and N. Furman (eds.),
           *Women and Language in Literature and Society*. New York: Praeger.
           157-173.
  1988.    "Cooperation and Competition Across Girls' Play Activities." In S.
           Fisher and A. Todd (eds.), *Gender and Discourse: The Power of Talk*.
           Norwood, NJ: Ablex Publishing Company. 55-94.
Grice, H.P.
  1975.    "Logic and Conversation. " In P. Cole and J. Morgan (eds.), *Syntax and
           Semantics 3: Speech Acts*. New York: Academic Press. 41-58.
Grimshaw, A. (ed.)
  1990.    *Conflict Talk*. Cambridge: Cambridge University Press.
Gumperz, J.
  1964.    "Linguistic and Social Interaction in Two Communities." In John
           Gumperz and Dell Hymes (eds.) "The Ethnography of Communication."
           *American Anthropologist*, 66:6, pt. II. 137-154.
  1972a.   "Communication in Multilingual Societies." In S. Tyler (ed.), *Cognitive
           Anthropology*. New York: Holt, Rinehart and Winston.
  1972b.   Introduction. In John Gumperz and Dell Hymes (eds.), *Directions in
           Sociolinguistics*. Oxford: Basil Blackwell. 1-25.
  1974.    "Linguistic Anthropology in Society." *American Anthropologist*, 76.
           785-98.

1977.    "Sociocultural Knowledge in Conversational Inference." In M.
         Saville-Troike (ed.) *28th Annual Round Table Monograph Series on
         Language and Linguistics*. Washington, D.C.: Georgetown University
         Press.

1982.    *Discourse Strategies*. Cambridge: Cambridge University Press.

1989.    "Interpretative Method in the Study of Urban Language." Lecture,
         University of Berne, Symposium, Verbale Kommunikation in der Stadt.
         October 2, 1989. Berne, Switzerland.

Gumperz, J. and Hymes, D. (eds.).

1964.    "The Ethnography of Communication." *American Anthropologist* 66:6,
         pt. II.

1972,1986. *Directions in Sociolinguistics*. Oxford: Basil Blackwell.

Harman, L.

1988.    *The Modern Stranger*. Berlin: Mouton de Gruyter.

Harrigan, J.A.

1980.    "Methods of Turn-taking in Group Interaction." *Papers from the
         Sixteenth Regional Meeting Chicago Linguistic Society*. April 17-18.
         102-111.

Heller, M. (ed.).

1988.    *Codeswitching*. Berlin: Mouton de Gruyter.

Hockett, C.

1958.    *A Course in Modern Linguistics*. New York: Macmillan.

Hudson, R.A.

1980.    *Sociolinguistics*. Cambridge: Cambridge University Press.

Hymes, D.

1962.    "The Ethnography of Speaking." In T. Gladwin and W.C. Sturtevant
         (eds.), *Anthropology and Human Behavior*. Anthropological Society of
         Washington, Washington, D.C. 13-53.

1972.    "Models of the Interaction of Language and Social Life." In John
         Gumperz and Dell Hymes (eds.), *Directions in Sociolinguistics*. Oxford:
         Basil Blackwell. 35-71.

Johns-Lewis, C. (ed.).

1986.    *Intonation in Discourse*. London and Sydney: Croom Helm.

Katz, D. and Kahn, R.

1966.    *The Social Psychology of Organizations*. 2nd. Edition. New York: John
         Wiley & Sons.

Keenan, E.O. and Schieffelin, B.
   1976.    "Topic as a Discourse Notion: A Study of Topic in the Conversations of
            Children and Adults." In C. Li (ed.), *Subject and Topic*. New York:
            Academic Press. 337-384.
Kendon, A.
   1967.    "Some functions of gaze direction in social interaction." *Acta
            Psychologica*, 26. 22-63.
Kennedy, C.W. and Camden, C.T.
   1983.    "A New Look at Interruptions." *Western Journal of Speech
            Communication*, 47:1. 45-58.
Kochman, T.
   1981.    *Black and White Styles in Conflict*. Chicago and London: University of
            Chicago Press.
Labov, W.
   1966.    *The Social Stratification of English in New York City*. Arlington: Center
            for Applied Linguistics.
   1972a.   *Sociolinguistic Patterns*. Philadelphia: University of Pennsylvania Press.
   1972b.   *Language in the Inner City*. Philadelphia: University of Pennsylvania
            Press.
   1972c.   "On the Mechanism of Linguistic Change." In John Gumperz and Dell
            Hymes (eds.), *Directions in Sociolinguistics*. Oxford: Basil Blackwell.
            512-537.
Labov, W. and Fanshel, D.
   1977.    *Therapeutic Discourse*. Orlando, Florida: Academic Press.
Labov, W. and Waletsky, J.
   1967.    "Narrative Analysis: Oral Versions of Personal Experience." In J.Helm
            (ed.), *Essays On the Verbal and Visual Arts*. Seattle: University of
            Washington Press. 12-44.
Lakoff, R.
   1973.    "The Logic of Politeness; Or, Minding your p's and q's." In *Papers from
            the Ninth Regional Meeting of the Chicago Linguistic Society*. Chicago:
            University of Chicago Press. 292-305.
   1975.    *Language and Women's Place*. New York: Harper & Row.
   1989.    "The Limits of Politeness: Therapeutic and Courtroom Discourse."
            *Multilingua* 8:2/3. 101-129.
Lebra, T.S.
   1987.    "Silence in Japanese Communication." *Multilingua*, 6:4. 343-357.

Leech, G.
   1983.    *Principles of Pragmatics*. London: Longman.
Le Page, R.B. and Tabouret-Keller, A.
   1985.    *Acts of Identity. Creole-based Approaches to Language and Ethnicity*.
            Cambridge: Cambridge University Press.
Lukes, S.
   1974.    *Power: A Radical View*. London: The Macmillan Press, Ltd.
Mackey, W.F.
   1968.    "The Description of Bilingualism." In J. Fishman (ed.), *Readings in the
            Sociology of Language*. The Hague: Mouton. 554-84.
Maclay, H. and Osgood, C.
   1959.    "Hesitation Phenomena in Spontaneous English Speech." *Word*, 15.
            19-44.
Maltz, D. and Borker, R.
   1982.    "A Cultural Approach to Male-female Miscommunication." In J.
            Gumperz (ed.), *Language and Social Identity*, Cambridge: Cambridge
            University Press. 197-216.
Mannheim, K.
   1968.    *Ideology and Utopia*. New York: Harcourt Brace & World, Inc.
Mead, G.H.
   1934.    *Mind, Self and Society*. Chicago: University of Chicago Press.
Meltzer, L., Morris, W. and Hayes, D.
   1971.    "Interruption Outcomes and Vocal Amplitude: Explorations in Social
            Psychophysics." *Journal of Personality and Social Psychology*, 8:3.
            392-402.
Milroy, J.
   1981.    *Regional Accents of English: Belfast*. Belfast: Blackstaff.
Milroy, J. and Milroy, L.
   1978.    "Belfast; Change and Variation in an Urban Vernacular." In P. Trudgill
            (ed.), *Sociolinguistic Patterns in British English*. London: Arnold. 19-36.
   1985.    "Linguistic change. Social Network and Speaker Innovation." *Journal of
            Linguistics*, 21. 339-84.
Milroy, L.
   1980.    *Language and Social Networks*. Oxford: Basil Blackwell.
   1987.    *Observing and Analysing Natural Language*. Oxford: Basil Blackwell.

Mitchell, J.C.
  1969.   *Social Networks in Urban Situations.* Manchester: Manchester University Press.
Murray, S.O.
  1985.   "Toward a Model of Members' Methods for Recognizing Interruptions." *Language in Society*, 14. 31-40.
Natale, M., Entin, E. and Jaffe, J.
  1979.   "Vocal Interruptions in Dyadic Communication as a Function of Speech Social Anxiety." *Journal of Personality and Social Psychology*, 37. 865-878.
Philips, S.
  1976.   "Some Sources of Cultural Variability in The Regulation of Talk." *Language in Society*, 5. 81-95.
Polsby, N.W.
  1963.   *Community Power and Political Theory.* New Haven and London: Yale University Press.
Potter, J. and Wetherell, M.
  1987.   *Discourse and Social Psychology.* London: SAGE Publications.
Roberts, K., Cook, F.G., Clark, S.C. and Semeonoff, E.
  1977.   *The Fragmentary Class Struggle.* London: Heinemann.
Romaine, S.
  1989.   *Bilingualism.* Oxford: Basil Blackwell.
Sacks, H.
  1967.   "On Getting the Floor." Lecture 7, part 2, October 26, 1967. University of California, Irvine.
  1971.   Lecture Notes. School of Social Science, University of California at Irvine.
Sacks, H., Schegloff, E.A. and Jefferson, G.
  1974.   "A Simplest Systematics for the Organization of Turn-Taking in Conversation." *Language*, 50:4. 696-735.
Saks, M.J. and Krupat, E.
  1988.   *Social Psychology and its Applications.* New York: Harper and Row.
Sapir. E.
  1947.   *Language, Culture and Personality.* Berkeley: University of California Press.

Schattschneider, E.E.
    1960.    *The Semi-Sovereign People: A Realist's View of Democracy in America.* New York: Holt, Rinehart and Winston.

Schegloff, E.A.
    1968.    "Sequencing in Conversational Openings." *American Anthropologist*, 70. 1075-95.
    1979.    "The Relevance of Repair to Syntax-for-Conversation." In T. Givon (ed.), *Syntax and Semantics. vol. 12, Discourse and Syntax.* New York: Academic Press. 261-286.

Schegloff, E., Jefferson, G. and Sacks, H.
    1977.    "The Preference for Self-correction in the Organization of Repair in Conversation." *Language*, 53:1. 361-382.

Schegloff, E.A. and Sacks, H.
    1973.    "Opening up Closings." *Semiotica*, 8. 289-327.

Schein, E.
    1988.    *Organizational Psychology.* 3rd. Edition. Englewood Cliffs, N.J.: Prentice-Hall.

Scherer, K. and Giles, H. (eds.).
    1979.    *Social Markers in Speech.* Cambridge: Cambridge University Press.

Schiffrin, D.
    1987.    *Discourse Markers.* Cambridge: Cambridge University Press.

Scollon, R. and Scollon, S.
    1981.    *Narrative, Literacy and Face in Interethnic Communication.* Norwood, New Jersey: Ablex.

Searle, J.R.
    1969.    *Speech Acts.* Cambridge: Cambridge University Press.

Searle, J.R.
    1975.    "Indirect Speech Acts." In P. Cole, and J.L. Morgan, (eds.), *Syntax and Semantics 3: Speech Acts.* New York: Academic Press. 59-82.

Sperber, D. and Wilson, D.
    1986.    *Relevance. Communication and Cognition.* Cambridge, Mass.: Harvard University Press.

Stech, E.L.
    1982.    "The Analysis of Conversational Topic Sequence Structures." *Semiotica*, 39:1/2. 75-91.

Stubbs, M.
  1983.    *Discourse Analysis.* Chicago: University of Chicago Press.
Tannen, D.
  1981.    "The Machine-gun Question: An Example of Conversational Style."
            *Journal of Pragmatics,* 5. 383-397.
  1982.(ed.). *Analyzing Talk and Discourse: Text and Talk.* Washington, D.C.:
            Georgetown University Press.
  1984.    *Conversational style: Analyzing talk among friends.* Norwood, N.J.:
            Ablex.
  1987.    "Repetition in conversation as spontaneous formulaicity." *Text,* 7:3.
            215-243.
Trimboli, C. and Walker, M.B.
  1984.    "Switching Pauses in Cooperative and Competitive Conversations."
            *Journal of Experimental Social Psychology,* 20. 297-311.
Trudgill, P. (ed.)
  1978.    *Sociolinguistic Patterns in British English.* London: Arnold.
Tumin, M.
  1985.    *Social Stratification. The forms and functions of inequality.* Englewood
            Cliffs, N.J.: Prentice-Hall, Inc.
van Dijk, T. (ed.)
  1985.    *Handbook of Discourse Analysis. vol. 1, Disciplines of Discourse. vol. 3,
            Discourse and Dialogue. vol. 4, Discourse Analysis in Society.* London:
            Acadmic Press.
Watts, R.J.
  1989.    "Relevance and Relational Work: Linguistic Politeness as Politic
            Behavior." *Multilingua,* 8:2/3. 131-166.
  1991.    *Power in Family Discourse.* Berlin: Mouton de Gruyter.
  1992.    "Linguistic Politeness and Politic Verbal Behavior: Reconsidering
            Claims for Universality." In R. J. Watts, S. Ide and K. Ehrlich (eds.),
            *Politeness in Language: Studies in its History, Theory and Practice.*
            Berlin: Mouton de Gruyter.
Watzlawick, P., Beavin Bavelas, J., and Jackson, D.D.
  1967.    *Pragmatics of Human Communication.* New York: W.W. Norton &
            Company.

West, C.

   1979.    *Against our Will: Male Interruptions of Females in Cross-sex Conversations*. Annals of the New York Academy of Sciences, 327. 81-97.

West, C. and Zimmerman, D.

   1980.    "Conversation Analyses." In K. Scherer and P. Ekman (eds.), *Handbook of Methods in Nonverbal Behavior Research*. Cambridge: Cambridge University Press. 506-41.

Whorf, B.L.

   1957.    *Language, Thought, and Reality: Selected Writings of Benjamin Lee Whorf*. (edited by John. B. Carroll). Cambridge, Mass.: M.I.T. Press.

Whyte, W.F.

   1943.    *Street Corner Society*. Chicago: University of Chicago Press.

Yngve, V.

   1970.    "On Getting a Word in Edgewise." *Sixth Regional Meeting of the Chicago Linguistic Society*. Chicago, Ill.: University of Chicago Press. 567-577.

Zimmerman, D. and West, C.

   1975.    "Sex role, interruptions and silences in conversation." In B. Thorne and N.Henley, (eds.), *Language and Sex*. Rowley, Mass.: Newbury House. 105-29.

# Subject Index

# Author Index

Austin, J.L., 6

Bachrach, P. and Baratz, M., 13
Bales, R.F., 85, 87
Barnes, J.A., 32
Bateson, G., 125, 132
Bavelas, J., et al., 118, 125
Bereiter, C., Engleman, S., et al., 4
Bernstein, B., 35, 37, 121
Blom, J.P. and Gumperz, J.J., 23, 28, 30, 121
Boas, F., 27
Boissevain, J., 32, 33, 34, 35, 41
Bott, E., 32, 33
Boulding, K., 117, 120
Brown, G. and Yule, G., 5, 7n, 15, 52, 92
Brown, P. and Levinson, S., 7, 20, 48, 50, 52, 54, 56, 57, 58, 62, 65, 75, 76, 81, 118, 121, 146
Bublitz, W., 93, 95, 96, 96n, 118, 135
Butterworth, et al., 54

Chafe, W., 54
Cheshire, J., 4

Dahl, R.A., 13
Davis, K., 13, 14, 151
Dittman, A.T. and Llewellyn, L.G., 88, 90
Duncan, S., 87, 88
Duncan, S. and Fiske, D., 87
Duncan, S. and Niederere, G., 87
Durkheim, E., 19

Edelsky, C., 89, 96n, 138

Ferguson, N., 21n, 88, 91
Foucault, M., 14
French, P. and Local, J., 88

Geertz, C., 3
Goffmann, E., 7, 14, 17, 18, 20, 47, 48, 64, 119, 129, 134, 137, 143
Goldman-Eisler, F., 54
Goodwin, C. and Goodwin, M., 104, 107, 115, 121, 122, 123, 126, 153
Goodwin, M.H., 104
Grice, H.P., 6, 60, 143
Grimshaw, A., 118, 119, 120
Gumperz, J., 2, 23, 30, 31, 76, 144
Gumperz, J. and Hymes, D., 4, 7n, 7, 30

Harman, L., 2n
Heller, M., 23
Hockett, C., 92
Hudson, R.A., 22
Hymes, D., 7, 23n, 30

Katz, D. and Kahn, R., 133
Keenan, E.O. and Schieffelin, B., 92, 97
Kendon, A., 88
Kochman, T., 4, 119

Labov, W., 4, 10, 12, 28, 29, 33 36, 37, 38, 39, 43, 76, 80, 81, 121
Labov, W. and Fanshel, D., 2, 15, 113, 125
Lakoff, R., 2, 7, 14, 52, 121, 125
Leech, G., 7
Lukes, S., 12n, 150

In the PRAGMATICS AND BEYOND NEW SERIES the following titles have been published thus far:

1. WALTER, Bettyruth: *The Jury Summation as Speech Genre: An Ethnographic Study of What it Means to Those who Use it.* Amsterdam/Philadelphia, 1988.
2. BARTON, Ellen: *Nonsentential Constituents: A Theory of Grammatical Structure and Pragmatic Interpretation.* Amsterdam/Philadelphia, 1990.
3. OLEKSY, Wieslaw (ed.): *Contrastive Pragmatics.* Amsterdam/Philadelphia, 1989.
4. RAFFLER-ENGEL, Walburga von (ed.): *Doctor-Patient Interaction.* Amsterdam/Philadelphia, 1989.
5. THELIN, Nils B. (ed.): *Verbal Aspect in Discourse.* Amsterdam/Philadelphia, 1990.
6. VERSCHUEREN, Jef (ed.): *Selected Papers from the 1987 International Pragmatics Conference. Vol. I: Pragmatics at Issue. Vol. II: Levels of Linguistic Adaptation. Vol. III: The Pragmatics of Intercultural and International Communication* (ed. with Jan Blommaert). Amsterdam/Philadelphia, 1991.
7. LINDENFELD, Jacqueline: *Speech and Sociability at French Urban Market Places.* Amsterdam/Philadelphia, 1990.
8. YOUNG, Lynne: *Language as Behaviour, Language as Code: A Study of Academic English.* Amsterdam/Philadelphia, 1990.
9. LUKE, Kang-Kwong: *Utterance Particles in Cantonese Conversation.* Amsterdam/Philadelphia, 1990.
10. MURRAY, Denise E.: *Conversation for Action. The computer terminal as medium of communication.* Amsterdam/Philadelphia, 1991.
11. LUONG, Hy V.: *Discursive Practices and Linguistic Meanings. The Vietnamese system of person reference.* Amsterdam/Philadelphia, 1990.
12. ABRAHAM, Werner (ed.): *Discourse Particles. Descriptive and theoretical investigations on the logical, syntactic and pragmatic properties of discourse particles in German.* Amsterdam/Philadelphia, 1991.
13. NUYTS, Jan, A. Machtelt BOLKESTEIN and Co VET (eds): *Layers and Levels of Representation in Language Theory: a functional view.* Amsterdam/Philadelphia, 1990.
14. SCHWARTZ, Ursula: *Young Children's Dyadic Pretend Play.* Amsterdam/Philadelphia, 1991.
15. KOMTER, Martha: *Conflict and Cooperation in Job Interviews.* Amsterdam/Philadelphia, 1991.
16. MANN, William C. and Sandra A. THOMPSON (eds): *Discourse Description: Diverse Linguistic Analyses of a Fund-Raising Text.* Amsterdam/Philadelphia, 1992.
17. PIÉRAUT-LE BONNIEC, Gilberte and Marlene DOLITSKY (eds): *Language Bases ... Discourse Bases.* Amsterdam/Philadelphia, 1991.
18. JOHNSTONE, Barbara: *Repetition in Arabic Discourse. Paradigms, syntagms and the ecology of language.* Amsterdam/Philadelphia, 1991.
19. BAKER, Carolyn D. and Allan LUKE (eds): *Towards a Critical Sociology of Reading Pedagogy. Papers of the XII World Congress on Reading.* Amsterdam/Philadelphia, 1991.
20. NUYTS, Jan: *Aspects of a Cognitive-Pragmatic Theory of Language. On cognition, functionalism, and grammar.* Amsterdam/Philadelphia, 1992.

21. SEARLE, John R. et al.: *(On) Searle on Conversation*. Compiled and introduced by Herman Parret and Jef Verschueren. Amsterdam/Philadelphia, 1992.
22. AUER, Peter and Aldo Di LUZIO (eds): *The Contextualization of Language*. Amsterdam/Philadelphia, 1992.
23. FORTESCUE, Michael, Peter HARDER and Lars KRISTOFFERSEN (eds): *Layered Structure and Reference in a Functional Perspective. Papers from the Functional Grammar Conference, Copenhagen, 1990*. Amsterdam/Philadelphia, 1992.
24. MAYNARD, Senko K.: *Discourse Modality: Subjectivity, Emotion and Voice in the Japanese Language*. Amsterdam/Philadelphia, 1993.
25. COUPER-KUHLEN, Elizabeth: *English Speech Rhythm. Form and function in everyday verbal interaction*. Amsterdam/Philadelphia, 1993.
26. STYGALL, Gail: Trial Language. *A study in differential discourse processing*. Amsterdam/Philadelphia, 1994.
27. SUTER, Hans Jürg: *The Wedding Report: A Prototypical Approach to the Study of Traditional Text Types*. Amsterdam/Philadelphia, 1993.
28. VAN DE WALLE, Lieve: *Pragmatics and Classical Sanskrit*. Amsterdam/Philadelphia, 1993.
29. BARSKY, Robert F.: *Constructing a Productive Other: Discourse theory and the convention refugee hearing*. Amsterdam/Philadelphia, 1994.
30. WORTHAM, Stanton E.F.: *Acting Out Participant Examples in the Classroom*. Amsterdam/Philadelphia, 1994.
31. WILDGEN, Wolfgang: *Process, Image and Meaning. A realistic model of the meanings of sentences and narrative texts*. Amsterdam/Philadelphia, 1994.
32. SHIBATANI, Masayoshi and Sandra A. THOMPSON (eds): *Essays in Semantics and Pragmatics*. Amsterdam/Philadelphia, 1995.
33. GOOSSENS, Louis, Paul PAUWELS, Brygida RUDZKA-OSTYN, Anne-Marie SIMON-VANDENBERGEN and Johan VANPARYS: *By Word of Mouth. Metaphor, metonymy and linguistic action in a cognitive perspective*. Amsterdam/Philadelphia, 1995.
34. BARBE, Katharina: Irony in Context. Amsterdam/Philadelphia, 1995.
35. JUCKER, Andreas H. (ed.): *Historical Pragmatics. Pragmatic developments in the history of English*. Amsterdam/Philadelphia, 1995.
36. CHILTON, Paul, Mikhail V. ILYIN and Jacob MEY: *Political Discourse in Transition in Eastern and Western Europe (1989-1991)*. Amsterdam/Philadelphia, n.y.p.
37. CARSTON, Robyn, Nam SUN SONG and Seiji UCHIDA (eds): *Relevance Theory. Applications and implications*. Amsterdam/Philadelphia, n.y.p.
38. FRETHEIM, Thorstein and Jeanette K. GUNDEL (eds): *Reference and Referent Accessibility*. Amsterdam/Philadelphia, n.y.p.
39. HERRING, Susan (ed.): *Computer-Mediated Communication. Linguistic, social, and cross-cultural perspectives*. Amsterdam/Philadelphia, n.y.p.
40. DIAMOND, Julie: *Status and Power in Verbal Interaction. A study of discourse in a close-knit social network*. Amsterdam/Philadelphia, 1996.
41. VENTOLA, Eija and Anna MAURANEN, (eds): *Academic Writing. Intercultural and textual issues*. Amsterdam/Philadelphia, 1996.